Epilepsy

Gill Parkinson and Mike Johnson

continuum

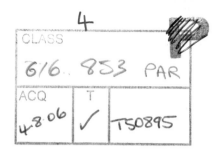
Continuum International Publishing Group

The Tower Building
11 York Road
London
SE1 7NX

80 Maiden Lane
Suite 704
New York
NY 10038

www.continuumbooks.com

© Gill Parkinson and Mike Johnson 2006

British Library Cataloguing-in-Publication Data
A catalogue record for this book is available from the British Library.

ISBN: 0–8264–8748–3 (paperback)

Library of Congress Cataloging-in-Publication Data
A catalog record for this book is available from the Library of Congress.

Typeset by BC Typesetting Ltd, Bristol BS31 1NZ
Printed and bound in Great Britain by
MPG Books Ltd, Bodmin, Cornwall

Contents

Contents

Acknowledgements

The authors would particularly like to thank all the families who took part in the study referred to in our book. We should also like to thank Epilepsy Action for permitting us to publish some of their material from their *Epilepsy Policy for Schools* (2005) and *Positive Action in Education* (2005).

Preface

This book aims to help teachers, parents, other professionals and pupils themselves understand epilepsy and its effects on families and schools. There are three ways in which epilepsy must be controlled – personally, medically and socially. It must be controlled personally because it is potentially a life-long condition. If it is not to take over a person's life it is important that they are always involved in and where possible make for themselves any decisions relating to that life. This includes medical decisions. Clearly, the skills and experience of doctors, consultants and specialist technicians will be needed to determine the type and severity of the epilepsy and, hopefully, what is causing it. However, the person themselves and their family must decide what balance they wish to strike between the control over their epilepsy that a particular drug can give and the side-effects they may experience or risk. Finally, the person must also decide how they are going to let the condition affect them socially and how they are going to react to and manage the responses of others.

This book gives clear, up-to-date, factual information about the condition and its treatment.

Preface

We also report the experiences of a large number of families who have successfully lived with epilepsy. In many cases they had to strive for this success and their comments should help readers to anticipate possible difficulties, and some solutions. We also detail the law relating to the support that schools can be expected to give and the protection from discrimination that is afforded by recent legislation.

We hope and expect that as a result of reading this book you will agree with one of the cases discussed that, 'They forget it – it sounds awful but it's true. But they don't forget because they know it's there, and that's that'.

Gill Parkinson and Mike Johnson
December 2005

1 Fits, Faints and Funny Feelings

Introduction

You may be asking yourself as you pick up this book, why do I need to know about epilepsy? You may have seen someone have a seizure (fit) on TV, or a young child with a high temperature – but why should it affect you? Well, for a start, epilepsy is more common than you might think. Many different sorts of people have epilepsy. It is the second most common neurological condition in children after migraine. It is more common in school-aged children than diabetes. The difference is that it tends to remain hidden. People have mixed views and misconceptions about what it is, what starts it off and how it can be kept under control. Over 80 per cent of children with active epilepsy have it under control most commonly by taking anti-epileptic drugs (AEDs).

Even though you may not have come into direct contact with epilepsy, the knowledge that your child or a child of someone you know or work with has epilepsy can initially be devastating and very frightening news. It will affect the child, his or her family and those who come into contact with the child through early years' services, school and beyond. To ensure that the child concerned has the best possible chance in life, it is important for all to become well informed about its causes, how it is treated and its impact on learning and behaviour.

This short book is intended as a 'one-stop-shop' guide to epilepsy in children and how we as parents, carers, teachers and service providers can ensure the child concerned has the best chance of a positive quality of life and opportunity alongside other children.

Although the book will inevitably contain some medical terms, we have tried to present information in a clear and accessible way, with the emphasis more on the social, psychological and educational implications of epilepsy for the child and the family, rather than concentrate on the more technical aspects of diagnostic procedures and treatment options. Where we have touched upon these aspects we have included suggestions for further reading and information sources that will provide you with more detailed information.

What is epilepsy?

The term 'epilepsy' comes from a Greek word meaning 'to take hold of' – hence the use of 'seizure' to describe its effects. Epilepsy may also be looked upon as a tendency to have repeated seizures. The seizures are an outward, visible sign that a part of the brain is not working as it should. Its activity of transmitting and receiving electrical and chemical messages becomes disrupted. The neurones (nerve cells) that carry messages around to different parts of the brain send them in a different order, or too strongly (excessive discharges). This results in the child having a seizure. The way in which a seizure affects what someone says, does or feels depends on where in the brain the problem is and how far the disruption spreads. A seizure can start by affecting one part of the brain and then spread to another part or even go on to affect the whole brain. This is why people can experience different types of seizure, lasting from a few seconds to several minutes.

Having epilepsy does not mean you are mentally ill or automatically have difficulties in learning, or have to take medicines for the rest of your life. Nor does it mean that if epilepsy happens in childhood it will stay with the child into adulthood. A substantial number of children grow out of their seizures as they enter adulthood; others may not encounter epilepsy until adolescence. Having epilepsy does not necessarily mean the child cannot live the way his or her friends live, or share in the same activities. Support arrangements may be needed in order for this to happen (this is explored later). While living with epilepsy is not easy, we actively encourage those involved with the child, and indeed the children themselves, to develop a positive attitude to their condition – looking at what it enables them to participate in and taking control of it, rather than viewing it as an illness or disabling condition that will blight the rest of their lives.

Parents often ask why their child has epilepsy and seem surprised when the doctor cannot give them a definite answer. This is because despite having carried out a range of diagnostic tests, which may include blood tests and brain scans of various kinds, taken a careful case history and looked at the electrical activity in the child's brain with an EEG (electroencephalogram), in up to 75 per cent of cases, there still might not be a definite answer to the question (see Appleton *et al.*, 2004, pp. 62–76 for a more detailed explanation of the strengths and limitations of EEGs and scans in epilepsy diagnosis and treatment planning). Children with this type of epilepsy are often described as having idiopathic epilepsies – where the cause is not known.

The most common causes of epilepsy are shown in Table 1.

Table 1

Most common causes of epilepsy in children:

- an infection in the brain, e.g. meningitis or encephalitis
- head injury
- if the brain is starved of oxygen, e.g. before or at birth
- part of a metabolic disorder
- the way the child's brain developed before birth
- recreational drugs or alcohol
- brain tumours
- part of an inherited condition, e.g. tuberous sclerosis, Rett syndrome, Angelman syndrome, Sturge-Weber syndrome, Fragile X syndrome, neurofibromatosis and Down's syndrome. (These syndromes all have websites where you can access more detailed and up-to-date information on the specific aspects.)

At least 10 per cent of children have a positive family history of seizures occurring with fever under the age of 5 years (febrile convulsions). However, the presence of such seizures (or convulsions) does *not* mean the child will necessarily go on to develop full-blown epilepsy.

Research in the field of genetics has shown recognizable links between certain conditions and the way in which they occur in families. This is not so surprising when you think of genes as mini instruction kits passed on from parents to their children. They are what give children their characteristics through instructing the 'new' cells how to work and behave together in deciding how tall they will be, the colour of their eyes and skin, etc. Like all the best-laid plans, this does not always work out as we would wish. For example, it is now generally recognized that 'primary generalized epilepsy' can run in families. Epilepsy genes fall into clear groups. They can cause:

- abnormal brain development
- progressive neurological degeneration (rare)
- disturbance in the way the brain metabolizes energy, or
- chemical transmission in the brain.

Photosensitive epilepsy may also have a genetic link in some instances. It is twice as common in girls as in boys. It occurs between the ages of 10 and 16 and usually stops at the end of adolescence.

Childhood absence epilepsy is a syndrome in which absences usually start when the child is between 2 and 12 years old. Although clearly shown by family studies to be of genetic origin, it is not due to a single gene defect but to a gene attachment to part (an arm) of chromosome 8q.

Epilepsy

Epilepsy is also found in association with other conditions, but not necessarily with definite genetic links. The most common ones are set out in Table 2.

Table 2

Common conditions with epilepsy as a feature:

- cerebral palsy (25–30%)
- autism and related disorders (about 30%)
- severe learning difficulties (up to 50%).

What *isn't* epilepsy?

More than one in ten of us will have a seizure at some point in our lives, but that does not mean that we will have epilepsy or necessarily be more predisposed to developing it than the next person. Therefore we need to be clear about what is not epilepsy so that we do not panic, or prejudge what is the matter with someone, should we witness or hear that they have had a seizure. Single seizures may happen for a range of reasons and usually occur when our systems are under stress, such as when we allow our blood sugar to fall too low through not having eaten for too long, or when we put our bodies under extreme physical stress as when climbing at altitude. Seizures can also occur (especially in young children) when the body has a high temperature (hence the name febrile seizures or convulsions). Excessive alcohol intake or drug-related effects can provoke seizures, but again these 'episodes' have to fulfil strict medical diagnostic criteria before a person may be given a diag-

Table 3

What is *not* symptomatic of epilepsy:

- jitteriness
- day-dreaming
- fainting (syncope)
- breath-holding episodes
- tics and ritualistic movements (mannerisms)
- night terrors
- visual disturbance or 'aura' associated with migraine
- sudden changes in colour, e.g. after trapping a finger
- jerks prior to onset of sleep.

---

nosis of epilepsy. If you are in any doubt about this, then you should visit your GP who will refer you for tests if it is relevant. Other conditions may be mistakenly thought of as seizures. These are set out in Table 3.

In order to make a diagnosis of epilepsy, however, the doctor will need many eyewitness accounts of 'episodes' that have occurred, to help make an accurate differential diagnosis between epilepsy and other potential conditions. Therefore, if you observe an 'episode' or 'event', it is extremely important that you write down a description of what you observed as soon as possible afterwards. Try and record what happened immediately before the event, what happened during it (and how long it lasted) and what happened afterwards. For instance, did the child recover immediately as if nothing untoward or unusual had happened? Did the child lose consciousness, and if so for approximately how long a period of time? Did the child recall afterwards what had happened? Was there any nausea, sickness, stomach upset or headache before or afterwards? All these types of observation are absolutely invaluable in helping the doctor gain a full and accurate picture of what might have triggered or caused the event. This is needed to ensure the best and most appropriate treatment and support may be provided for the child concerned, and also so that everyone may start to make plans for the child's future – in terms of access to teaching and learning as well as specialist medical and psychological services (this is discussed in more detail later).

Seizures

Seizures may sometimes be called fits, attacks or convulsions, but essentially they all refer to the same phenomenon – an altered chemical state in the brain that provokes it to produce an excessive amount of electrical discharges. These discharges may be localized to one part of the brain, start locally and then spread to the whole brain, or affect the whole brain (almost) simultaneously. This results in a malfunction in message transmission so messages may be sent inadvertently, in the wrong order, or not at all. Put simply, this may result in the child losing consciousness or exhibiting a reduced level of alertness, involuntary movements, a change in behaviour and/or speech. Some seizures such as tonic-clonic seizures (previously called 'grand mal') are easy to recognize as they are so dramatic.

Others are not so easy. Some are recognizable as seizures but difficult to put a name to (classify) because either they are so subtle in the way they happen, or they occur in an atypical or unusual way, such as momentary confusion or lapses in concentration. This is why it is so important to obtain an eyewitness account of events, or record them on video if at all possible.

Seizure triggers

We do not always know what sets off or 'triggers' a seizure. Triggers vary from child to child and some children may be susceptible to more than one trigger. Richard Appleton and John Gibbs (1998) list eight of the most common potential trigger factors:

1. flicker, flash or pattern induced (photosensitive)
2. reading
3. startle reflex
4. physical activity
5. eating
6. immersion in hot or cold water
7. doing mathematics or calculations.

Photosensitive epilepsy is the most common. Given the right intensity, frequency and length of exposure a child will probably experience either a myoclonic jerk (rather like the jerk you sometimes experience when falling asleep) or a tonic-clonic seizure with consequent loss of consciousness that may last from a few seconds to several minutes. Sometimes there is a family history of similar types of epilepsy, and these occur more often in girls than boys. These types of seizures tend to occur most often, though not exclusively, in children aged 10–18 years, fading as they go into their 20s. Photosensitive epilepsy is found only in younger children when they have 'asymptomatic' or 'cryptogenic' epilepsy, i.e. when a cause for the condition is not known or only suspected.

Types of seizure

Children may have one or several types of seizure (see Table 4, p. 12). These may be restricted to one part of the brain (partial or focal seizures), or affect the whole brain (generalized). They usually last between a few seconds and five minutes. Some people have an aura or warning before a seizure which can take the form of:

- thinking you can smell something strange
- hearing sounds
- a headache
- an odd sensation in your stomach
- experiencing other unusual sensations.

What follows depends on the type of seizure and the part of the brain that triggers it.

In **partial seizures**, the child will remain aware of their surroundings. However, they may experience one or more of the following:

- motor symptoms affecting all or part of a limb, e.g. a shaking arm
- a chewing motion, plucking at clothes or walking round in circles
- talking to themselves

- somato-sensory or special sensory symptoms, e.g. butterflies in stomach or experiencing an odd smell
- psychic symptoms, e.g. a hallucination (seeing shapes or coloured lights).

Afterwards the child may feel upset or disorientated and need reassurance.

Occasionally a **complex partial seizure** (where consciousness is impaired but not completely lost) may turn into a tonic-clonic seizure. This is called a **complex partial with secondary generalization** because the abnormal electrical discharges have spread from one part of the brain to involve the whole brain.

There are six types of **generalized seizures** which involve the whole brain. These are set out in Table 4.

A child may have more than one kind of seizure at any one time, or may have one type of seizure when young and another when he/she goes into adolescence. Some children grow out of their epilepsy altogether. This is another reason why it is so important to ensure the correct diagnosis is made as early as possible.

If a child for whom you care or are responsible has epilepsy, then you should find out:

- the type of seizures the child experiences
- their frequency and whether they occur nocturnally (at night) or at specific times of the day, week or month
- any potential trigger factors, e.g. watching TV or a film, certain types of lighting, or an association with hunger, fatigue, changes in activity

Table 4 Classification of seizures

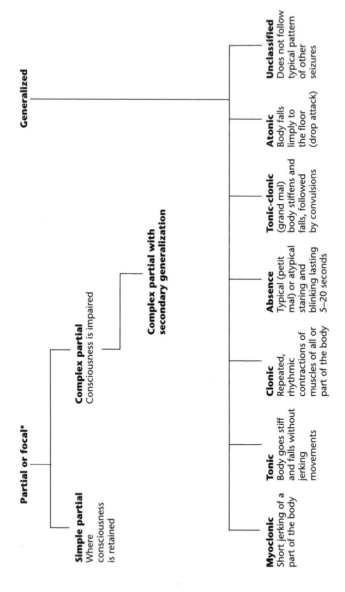

- how the seizure should be dealt with should it occur (this is discussed later).

Only a brief description of the main seizure type is provided here. You are recommended to read Appleton and Gibbs's excellent book *Epilepsy in Childhood and Adolescence.*

For more detailed descriptions, medical background and current management issues, refer to the Useful addresses at the end of this book. New treatments and guidance on childhood epilepsy are emerging all the time and while this book is the most up-to-date guide as we go to press, we do recommend that for more specific information you contact one of the associations listed or visit one of the national epilepsy websites such as Epilepsy Action.

Treatment for epilepsy

There are several forms of treatment for epilepsy and epileptic seizures. Most children take tablets or medicine and their epilepsy is usually well controlled. If you are a teacher or carer you should find out what treatment the child or young person is having. This is important for several reasons. The people responsible for the child need to know:

- how long the child has been on the current medication;

- whether special arrangements need to be made for pills to be taken during the day, e.g. while at school or play-group;
- arrangements for medical help which may be required if:
  - they experience a seizure longer than they would normally
  - breathing becomes impaired
  - the child does not recover from one seizure before going into another. When a child goes into this state (a rare medical condition), it is called status epilepticus (see section on management of medicines in schools, p. 89);
- what side-effects the pills (may) have;
- recent or forthcoming plans for changes in the treatment. This is important because changes may have an effect on academic performance, participation in physical activities or increased susceptibility to seizures until the child becomes accustomed to the new treatment.

When there are changes made in treatment, to the amount, type and times of taking drugs, you may be asked to watch for any changes in the child or young person while they are with you. Sometimes this can be difficult, especially as you may not always be sure what you are supposed to be watching for. Nevertheless, your observations assist the doctors, nurses and other professionals involved in case management make correct and, importantly, informed decisions that help maintain or improve that child's quality of life, learning and potential achievement.

The most useful information concerns any seizures you may witness. There are several features concerning the lead up to a seizure, how it begins and what follows, which provide useful evidence on which medical, social and educational management decisions can be made. One of the best and most efficient ways of recording such information in a logical and methodical manner is by using a Seizure Record Chart (see Table 5).

What should you do if a child in your care has a seizure? Read the following example of Martin aged 10, described by a member of staff on playground duty at lunch-time. Martin has epilepsy, but has never been known to have a seizure at school.

It is a bright and sunny afternoon. Martin is playing outside school with his friends. His friend comes running up to the member of staff on playground duty. 'I need you to come quickly,' calls Martin's friend, 'something has happened to Martin.' They find Martin at the edge of the path. He is making gurgling and grunting sounds in his throat. His arms and legs are jerking. His face has gone very pale and he is sweating. The member of staff gently rolls Martin onto one side and places a folded sweatshirt she had borrowed from another child under his head. She looks round to make sure Martin's arms and legs are not near any hard objects. She knows from the guidelines provided by the school not to try and put anything in Martin's mouth as it would do more harm than good. Gradually the seizure subsides.

The member of staff remains beside Martin. She realizes that Martin may feel tired and possibly a little confused once the seizure is over and need reassurance about what has happened. The member of staff asks one of the other children to call another member of staff and for a wheelchair to be brought out, so they can take Martin to a quieter, less public area of the school to recover.

When this has been organized, the member of staff fills out a Seizure Record Sheet. She is not certain what sort of seizure she has witnessed so she ticks the 'Unclassified' box on the Record Sheet. She carefully notes the length of time the seizure has lasted – approximately two minutes, though it seemed a lot longer while it was happening. Looking at Martin's school records she notes that although Martin does not need any Rescue Medication, his parents like to be notified if an 'episode' happens during the school day. Martin's mother was grateful his school had not felt the need to call the emergency services and said she would call and pick Martin up before school finished for the afternoon. Although Martin was tired and had a headache on returning home, he had no further seizures and went to school as usual the following day.

You may have noticed several points about what actions need to be taken if you witness someone in your care having a seizure.

1. Stay calm – not always easy when you are surrounded by other children, when you are out in a public place such as a shopping centre, park or in a swimming pool.

2. Move any objects like chairs or tables away so the child does not hurt themself inadvertently.
3. If the person concerned is unconscious, turn them on their side. If they are jerking head, arms and legs, place something soft under their head and ensure limbs are not caught on hard objects or furniture.
4. *Never* try to insert something in their mouth.
5. Note the time the seizure started and finished even if this is only approximate.
6. If the seizure seems longer than usual – say by two or more minutes, if breathing seems to be difficult and/or if the person goes into another seizure before fully recovering consciousness from the first one, summon medical assistance quickly. Lack of oxygen for any length of time to the brain can alter its metabolism, putting it at risk of damage should the situation continue untreated.
7. Discourage others from gathering around someone when they come round from a seizure.
8. If necessary cover the person having the seizure if you have a rug or blanket near at hand, as they will be embarrassed if they have been incontinent during their seizure.
9. As soon as possible seek help to move them to a more appropriate location.
10. If possible, clear any mess away as soon as you can to avoid further embarrassment.
11. Make sure either you or someone the person recognizes stays with them to reassure them when they regain consciousness. (They are likely to be quite

disorientated and may be unaware of what has happened at first.)

12. Do not give them any food or drink until they have fully come round.

13. As soon as possible after the event make a note of what happened
    a) just before the seizure occurred
    b) during the seizure
    c) immediately after, including how long it took for the person to recover (see Children's Seizure Record Chart in Table 5).

Other treatments for epilepsy

There are a variety of alternative treatment options becoming increasingly available as our knowledge about the brain, its chemical composition and functioning continues to develop and improve. The most well-known alternative to medication treatment is surgery. However, the child's epilepsy must accord with very specific criteria before surgery is considered a viable option, and only 4–6 per cent of *all* cases of epilepsy are thought to be suitable candidates for surgery. There needs to be clear and unambiguous evidence that seizures arise from a localized or focal area of the brain which is accessible and that there would be no damage to that person functionally once the offending part of the brain was removed.

Professionals involved with the care, support and teaching of children under consideration for surgery are often asked to provide examples of current academic, cognitive, linguistic and other skills and abilities. Combined with other tests, this information will help the surgical team, together with the child and his or her parents, decide whether the benefits outweigh the risks of an operation.

Vagal nerve stimulators (VNS), rather like pacemakers, have been tried in small-scale studies of children. The principle behind the VNS, as the name indicates, stimulates a nerve (the vagus) involved in sending and receiving messages from the brain. Although the underlying mechanism is uncertain, it is thought that the stimulation inhibits the onset of seizures. However, there is still much more research to be done in this area before conclusions can be drawn about its usefulness in children. Hoarseness and sometimes coughing were noted as side-effects in some VNS patients (Appleton and Gibbs, 1998). It remains to be established exactly which children and which types of epileptic seizure and syndromes would benefit from this form of treatment regime.

Other therapies include:

- acupuncture
- diets, e.g., ketogenic (very high fat) diet (variable success rate)
- behavioural therapies
- herbal, homeopathic and aromatherapy treatments.

For more detailed information on alternative therapies, contact the British Complementary Medicines Association or the Institute for Complementary Medicine.

Table 5 Children's Seizure Record Chart

Child's details	Name	DOB ....../ ....../ ....
	Place	Date....................
	Witnesses.....................................	Time......................
Before the seizure	Did anything make you think a seizure was going to happen? (e.g. illness, pre-seizure or preictal behaviour etc.)	
Immediate triggers or antecedents	What happened just before? (e.g. an argument, tantrum, stressful event, period of physical activity, watching TV, a fall etc.)	

continued on next page

Table 5 continued

Course of seizure	What did you see happen *first?* (e.g. loss of consciousness, muscle tone or posture, jerking, side and body parts involved, repetitive movements, colour change, slowed or nonsensical speech, change in behaviour, mobility, incontinence, etc.)
Treatment given and response	*(If drugs used give name, route (e.g. by mouth) and timing of administration and response)*
Post-ictal phase and recovery	How was the child after the seizure? (e.g. sleeping, confused, wandering, behaviour, balance, etc.)
	How long to full recovery?

continued on next page

Table 5 continued

Duration	How long did the seizure last?
Other comments	
Staff seizure classification	What sort of seizure do you think this is?
Notification	Time at which parent or next of kin notified. Any further action required and by whom
For use by medical staff	

Table 6 Most common medicines used for epilepsy

Generic name	Brand name
Phenobarbitone/phenobarbitol	Phenobarbitol
Phenytoin	Epanutin
Primidone	Mysoline
Ethosuximide	Emeside/Zarontin
Clonazepam	Rivotril
Clobazam	Frisium
Carbamazepine	Tegretol or tegretol retard
Sodium valproate or slow release s.v.	Epilim or Epilim Crono
Vigabatrin	Sabril
Lamotrigine	Lamictal
Gabapentin	Neurontin
Topiramate	Topamax
Tiagabine	Gabatril
Levetirasetan	Keppra
Lorazepam	Ativan
Acetazolamide	Diamox
Midazolam (for buccal or intranasal use only)	Epistat
Diazepam	Stesolid (for rectal use only)
Felbamate	Oxcarbazepine

Epilepsy in adolescence

Appleton and Gibbs (1998) quote figures of 75 teen-agers per 100,000 having their first seizure in adolescence, with prevalence rates of 6–7/1000. Partial (focal) epilepsies are known to start after puberty, as are some of the idiopathic generalized epilepsies. The causes of epilepsy in adolescence are not dissimilar to those found in younger children, although tumours are thought to be more common, as is the risk from substance and alcohol abuse.

With this group of young people one needs to be aware that what may be witnessed or reported to you as a seizure may not be epilepsy, but may be related to another condition such as:

- migraine
- syncope (fainting)
- panic attack
- substance abuse (especially cocaine, ecstasy, heroin and 'smack')
- pseudo-seizures or non-epileptic attack disorder.

Investigations used to make a differential diagnosis are similar to those used with younger children. Other professionals including teachers and parents may be asked to provide information on the following in order to help make an accurate diagnosis:

- any predisposing or antecedent factors which might precipitate a seizure, e.g. dappled sunlight, strobe lighting, relaxation after a PE lesson
- any family history of epilepsy
- incidence and frequency of headaches
- deterioration in academic performance
- personality changes beyond what one would normally associate with onset of puberty
- changes in attention, vigilance and concentration
- changes in behaviour and mood that appear 'out of the ordinary'
- suspicion of drug or alcohol abuse

- evidence of an erratic lifestyle felt to be out of character with previous behaviour.

Principles of treatment are similar to childhood epilepsy, although management in secondary school and FE/HE settings is slightly different because the person is older and the environments more complex. Issues concerning self-medication and taking responsibility for their own medicine administration are important aspects in adolescence – as with children with asthma or diabetes. Taking responsibility for self-medication helps the young person psychologically because it enables them to feel they have control of their epilepsy rather than the reverse. This is why psychological support for teenagers with epilepsy is as important as physical and medical support. It can tend to be overlooked by service providers, although some specialist epilepsy clinics and hospital out-patient services are addressing this issue in an effort to make sure pills are taken regularly, thus reducing the need for emergency admissions to hospital. This group of young people will require support from specialist epilepsy nurses, clinical psychological and possibly psychiatric services rather than standard neurology or specialist epilepsy (Sapphire) nurse practitioners.

It is the carer's responsibility to remain informed, to liaise and exchange information with relevant colleagues and parents, and to ensure the child or young person remains central in our efforts to provide support through the stages of assessment, diagnosis, treatment and management of the child or young person with epilepsy.

References

Appleton, R., Chappell, B. and Beirne, M. (2004) *Your Child's Epilepsy*, second edition. London, Classic Publishing.

Appleton, R. and Gibbs, J. (1998) *Epilepsy in Childhood and Adolescence*, second edition. London, Martin Dunitz.

2 Does This Child Have a Problem?

Johnson and Thomas (1998) financed by the then British Epilepsy Association (now Epilepsy Action) interviewed over 50 families who had a child with epilepsy. They also spoke with a sample of their GPs, consultants, school heads, Special Educational Needs Coordinators (SENCOs) and teachers. This chapter and Chapter 3 are based directly on the results of that investigation. The opinions stated are those of the investigators and do not necessarily represent those of Epilepsy Action.

Our aim is to let teachers know what a very representative sample of parents felt about their experiences with professionals as a result of having a child with epilepsy. We do not suggest that these are necessarily typical. We do suggest that it will be useful for professionals in both health and education to consider them and note the fairly simple measures that can be taken to improve parents' experiences. Teachers in particular need to know what the family is likely to have gone through during and after the process of diagnosis.

Chapter 1 described what epilepsy is and isn't. It has to be diagnosed in the true sense of the word. An adult (parent/carer or teacher) notices that there is 'something wrong' and the parent take the child to their GP who refers the child to a hospital consultant, preferably a paediatric neurologist, who arranges for tests, and if the results confirm the GP's suspicions they will prescribe an appropriate course of drugs and pass the case back to the GP for monitoring. The local school health service should be notified and the child's school given advice about day-to-day handling and any likely effects on school activities.

Two circulars, one relating to medical conditions, the other to special educational needs (SEN), govern the in-school support. If the family lives in the right place they may be given the support of a specialist nurse who may be funded by Epilepsy Action. These are called 'Sapphire Nurses' (see www.epilepsy.org.uk/services/sapphire.html). People with epilepsy now also have the protection of the Disability Discrimination Act (DDA) (1995). We will return to these rights and protections in Chapter 3.

Some consultants believe the need for drugs may diminish or disappear in late adolescence. The parents' opinions suggest this occurs less frequently than one might hope. It is a rare condition and few teachers have had personal experience of it. This can lead to fear as teachers don't know what is happening to the child and how best to cope with it.

It is quite clear that it is the *family* that 'has' epilepsy, not just the child. The family have to learn how to restructure their lives and expectations around that fact. Teachers need to make sure that they do not put unnecessary barriers in the way of the child's full participation in school life. Experiences during diagnosis are an important part of that learning and we hope that this book will help both teachers and parents to make the most of it.

First contact: the general practitioner

GP appointments are expected to take up approximately 10 minutes for each patient. For epilepsy, 30 minutes is more reasonable. The way the GP deals with this time-dilemma is important. If parents think they are being rushed (or are conscious of a full waiting room!) they should ask for another appointment to talk about it further.

GPs always refer the child to a consultant if they suspect epilepsy. They don't have the technology or the experience either to get or to interpret the information needed. However, if the consultant confirms that the symptoms are caused by epilepsy, it is the GP who will treat the child and monitor the effects of that treatment.

GPs' reasons for referring children to hospital:

'We just don't see enough cases to be able to justify looking after them properly ourselves. It just isn't on. The investigations and everything need to be run at secondary if not tertiary level, I think. Secondary, certainly.'

'I think that's a point more for a neurologist to explore or, you know, a paediatrician. I would expect them to pick up on that kind of thing and really to determine exactly, you know, if it was epilepsy and the investigations required, and the treatment, then to look at that side of things.'

What the GP can do, either now or at a future appointment, is discuss what will happen at the hospital and, possibly, implications for the future.

Some GPs handled this difficult situation well, according to parents' experiences:

'He just examined her and sort of said, he was pretty sure that it was a fit but he wasn't going to commit himself until she has tests and things done. But he was lovely.'

'He said that he thought that it was some form of epilepsy, that Ben was showing the signs that he might have epilepsy, but that to be sure he would have to send us to see Mr Brown so that he could make sure that that was what it was.'

These parents were given confidence in their GP's basic competence and understanding about epilepsy and its initial diagnosis. They also understood the need to refer to the hospital to confirm this.

Other families were not so fortunate:

'He didn't say why he was sending him for tests and, um, and I got really worried and thinking all sorts, sorts of . . . um, could he be looking for a tumour or something like that?'

'I went to the doctor because of what the school had told me and I was starting to, you know, get really worried about what could be wrong with her, you know, it could've been something really bad, um and he just told me that she needed to see a specialist and have tests, . . . no explanation, but [pause] then again I don't suppose I asked.'

This last statement is important. *Neither a teacher nor a parent should be afraid to ask.* This is when it is probably better to have another appointment. Parents can go to it having got over the initial shock and having thought about the questions they want to ask. Again the best advice is, 'Write them down!' That way they will have a checklist and the appointment will be more under their control. Also, *write down the answers.* That way you will all be able to talk about what was said rather than arguing about what it was!

Two questions that should always be asked are:

1. What sort of hospital is it that we are being referred to and do they specialize in treating children?
2. Is the consultant a *paediatric* neurologist?

The answers are important, as how the tests are carried out is nearly as important as what the results show.

The hospital experience can range from the positive to the traumatic. Specialist children's hospitals handle the situation best. However, some families are actually referred to psychiatric units.

'. . . When we went to this EEG place at [X], we walked in and it was sort of like, like a mental sort of place, and there was like rooms, and there were people wandering around. Um, and the patients were all walking around . . . and it was not a nice place to be in at all . . . It was very frightening actually. Even though we were walking through it with staff . . . and when you've first found out about it [that your child might have epilepsy] it's all a bit, you start to think what effect it will have on his mind, and will he end up somewhere like this?'

At the children's hospital it was very different:

'The total difference in the staff was amazing, they were so geared up to children and to calm down really frightened parents. It was very good and the consultant was a very good doctor as well.'

'And it was a contrast when we went to the children's hospital. You couldn't have had a bigger difference; the atmosphere was so, so much better. I mean they were really geared up to talking to John and they had the odd little toys in the room and it was a completely different atmosphere altogether. And I was a lot happier then and John was fine.'

In spite of the current political rhetoric of 'choice', parents may have to be quite firm about having a say in where their child is referred to. There is a lot of information available, both on the Internet and in your local library, giving details of hospitals in your area. Everyone should use it.

Experiences of having tests

Some children can be seen only as 'cases':

> 'I wasn't very impressed with her, because she was only young and it is quite frightening. I know it doesn't hurt, but I felt her remarks, such as "Let's see if there are any brains in your head" were insensitive – Mary took everything literally and was quite concerned about that. I didn't expect that from a professional who was actually doing the EEG. So I think we've had quite a lot of bad.'

> 'Nothing was explained, I mean, no, at the very beginning nothing was explained, because we'd actually seen a programme, on television, about the spike.'

Others were treated like intelligent human beings:

> 'The most helpful person we actually came across was the lady who took the EEG at Alder Hey, because she processes so many people and she was really good. You know, she told us what she was doing.'

> 'Yes, he explained, like, what goes on in their head, when they're either coming up to have a seizure or, and he explained, all the different seizures, what they

can have, and how it, like, affects them after, and stuff like that. I mean, he was really good, he was really, that part, he was brilliant, explaining.'

The visit to the hospital is the start of understanding the diagnosis and its implications. Anything that is said about how the child will be affected is a matter of probabilities. Epilepsy is not like having measles or a broken leg. It is an imbalance in a very delicate system and needs continual monitoring. How it affects the child is also a matter of psychology as well as pharmacology!

Seeing the consultant

The next step is to see the consultant. This is what the parents have been waiting for, to know the best or the worst. They need to develop a mutual understanding with the medical staff. They should tell them when they don't understand. In particular, parents need to know what is the best they can hope for and what is the worst that can happen. (This is never as bad as they have been imagining!) They can then report on their next visit to the hospital or doctor where, between these two, developments have been.

Some consultants might not translate 'medical' language:

'I mean, he could explain these big words quite easily, but just someone like a common housewife, you know, it's over the top. I think, sometimes I think they ought to talk to you instead of at you.'

Others can have a distant, superior attitude:

> 'Yes, Mr . . . , who was the consultant, I can't think of his name now. And he sort of looked down on you, sort of, parent, paranoid parent sort of thing, you know. Wouldn't explain anything.'

> 'His attitude, his body language, everything just said it. You know . . . and sometimes I felt so intimidated by that, I didn't ask. We used to come away and I had a thousand things I needed to ask him. Queries I wanted, you know, and things I wanted to say, but I just felt so intimidated. In actual fact, for a long time after we had that sort of fall-out, um, my confidence in myself, as Fiona's mother, was shaken, because I started to think, well maybe I don't know what I'm talking about and maybe there isn't anything wrong with her.'

> '. . . because of the way that he was, he didn't really make me feel like I could ask a great deal of questions, to talk about things, he had spoken and that was it really.'

There is a difference between being an expert and using that expertise. Again, encourage parents to write down their questions and make sure they understand the answers. If the consultant won't answer questions – they should be asked who will!

Most consultants communicate things very clearly:

'. . . he explained it very clearly to us and whatever questions we asked he answered and continually said to us, you know, whatever you don't take in now, come back to me . . . and we felt very comfortable.'

'We thought that he was very good because we always felt that we could ask him things, you know little things, that were not really that important, but that we wanted to know for our own peace of mind.'

These are examples of really good practice. It is important always to think about what has been said and see if it makes sense in the family's real world. Sooner or later parents, schools and children will have to develop their own ways of coping.

Remember again there is also plenty of information on the Internet and in the library. Trying to use this first might not only remove the need for a special appointment but could also result in you being equipped with 'better questions' when seeing the consultant.

Fortunately some schools and consultants have specialist nurses called Sapphire Nurses, paid for by Epilepsy Action. Their job is to liaise with parents and other agencies. Their aim is to give the security of having someone there to help understand and cope with the condition, to discuss and explore medical and wider issues and implications in more depth:

'I think she's just basically, if for some reason the consultant or the doctor doesn't put something so clear, she can come and see the family in their own surroundings, sit down, I mean she's been here for lunch and we go through everything that I've ever been concerned about. Or about us as a family or at school.'

'It's just so nice to be able to talk to her about all the little things that you are worried about . . . She's always there at the end of the phone if I need her, even if it's for something really silly, she always encourages me to call.'

A 'real world' understanding of anything is about the 'silly things', the personal feelings. Everyone needs to chat, talk about the 'little things', 'even if it's something silly', with someone so that they don't feel alone.

Once the diagnosis is clear, good information is needed about drugs. On the one hand taking the tablets should become as routine as cleaning teeth. On the other the chemicals they contain are affecting the brain and can have quite severe side-effects in some children. If parents and teachers don't know what the side-effects might be they can't know whether any behavioural changes seen come from the child's response to their condition, a side-effect of the drugs, or the manner in which their epilepsy manifests itself. Things can become very confusing:

'They said there's side-effects, and you do think and watch out for the hair loss and things like that.'

'The effects of the drugs were talked about so we knew, you know, if we had changes in the drugs that he might be sleepy, and things like that.'

Epilepsy

You can't assume that the hospital will think about this.

'Well, we started to get really worried about her behaviour, I mean she changed completely, she became really aggressive, no one said this could happen if she took those drugs.'

'At no point were we told about the side-effects of medication, they weren't discussed with me. I thought that our consultant, Mr Green, would have told me about that if it was a worry. But he tends to be the type of person who always says, "We'll cross that bridge when we come to it".'

If better or more detailed information is needed the hospital or GP may have booklets that might help or, again, there's always the Internet:

'You see, the thing is, people can tell you things, but it's hit or miss whether you actually take it in, isn't it? That's why literature is so good, because you can come away, and when you've got over the shock of the conversation, you can sit down and read about it.'

'We found the information not very well forthcoming, you know. Any information we've had, we've really had to fight for. Um, I'm really not sure where the line divides between a petit mal and a grand mal, so it's really difficult to explain to anybody else about it.'

Does This Child Have a Problem?

In spite of the fact that the medical and educational services are supposed to talk to each other it will probably be parents who have to pass on information to the school. Teachers need to know what signs and symptoms they should be paying attention to, and reporting back to parents about. They also need to be aware of how to minimize the effects of the epilepsy on learning and education, particularly now that they have enhanced responsibilities under the Special Educational Needs and Disability Act (SENDA). Parents need to make sure they are clear about what teachers need to know:

> 'Um, when we found out that he was epileptic, and he was diagnosed, we went up and explained as best we could, as best we knew, anyway, to the teacher and the headmaster. It was absolutely hopeless, because I couldn't explain to them.'

What parents need

So, first and foremost, parents need to have their child's epilepsy fully explained, with practical information about the condition and ways of dealing with it:

> 'Just what it is and how you go about dealing with it, you know.'

> 'Somebody who could give us, tell us what epilepsy was. You know, just to sort of say, well this is epilepsy, this is how you cope with it.'

39

Epilepsy

'You know, that's what you needed, really, just someone to say, epilepsy is this, this is what happens, this
is the result, you know, you can live a normal life.
You – you'd have got on with life better, really.'

Again, it's the little, silly things that matter:

'We would have liked to have known exactly, at that
moment in time, because I think it would have
stood us in good stead to be able to manage Eric's
way of life. Because I mean you can't put him on a
push-bike, this sort of thing. And it would have been
nice to say well, will he be safe to go on a push-
bike? What type of fit will he have? Is he safe in front
of lights? We've never been told any of this.'

'So, everyday things, you know, everyday worries. It
would have been nice to be able to talk them over
with somebody really.'

It's also those 'everyday things' that affect the family's
life continually. Firstly the child has to come to terms
with the diagnosis and any fits. Some handle it well:

'She does mention it. But she handles, handles it very
well, I think. And she, oh, the first thing she always
says when she's had a fit, the first thing she says is
"I'm all right, Mum, I'm all right". She's really
grown-up about it.'

'David was never upset by it. Once we'd explained what it was, I think he quite enjoyed it at one time, getting all the fuss.'

Others have difficulties:

'At first he was frightened, because he didn't really understand what it meant, you know, he probably thought, "what's going to happen to me". He said "is it something with my brain, or . . .". You know, he even asked "Am I going to die?" And I was just, "Don't worry, it's just a minor thing". I told him that his brain stops working for a couple of seconds, and then it starts up again, and now he accepts it.'

'Every so often she had a little sort of attack of "why me" and "it's not really happening to me", and she "forgets" to take her tablets.'

Some are frustrated or feel powerless:

''Cos I'm still, I'm not allowed to go to many places and it's not fair. Everyone gets to go to the disco. The other day there was a disco, this Friday, and everyone in the whole school went, except me.'
(We suspect that this would have been unlawful, now, under the DDA.)

Unfortunately, some schools not recognizing these feelings are less than helpful and make the child feel very different and excluded.

Epilepsy

'At one stage, he had a woman – when the statement finally come through – there was a nice lady up at the school, and this is what his statement involved, who followed him from lesson to lesson, to make sure he was safe. I can understand that, I suppose it's very helpful, but it just didn't work. He was determined that this woman was not going to follow him round in front of his mates and . . . wasn't just walking round with the crowd, she was – I think she was actually segregating him and making him walk holding hands. And teenagers do not want to hold hands . . . he was getting more and more alienated from the lads around him, which was then having this knock-on effect of the bullying and anything else – the Mickey-taking, yes, because kids are cruel, they're really, really cruel.'

Teachers should encourage parents to talk to their child about the day at school just in an interested fashion to stop this sort of stupidity before it does real harm. Bullying should *never* be allowed to pass unreported. A response of the type 'Boys will be boys' is totally unacceptable. It's the school's job to support and protect *all* its pupils.

Epilepsy can also lead to family dilemmas.

'But, when you're out, you tend to watch that one more than the little ones, you know what I mean, whereas you should be watching the little uns, and not the biggest one. But your mind's constantly sort of – "where is she, she hasn't wandered off", you know, in case she's had a black-out and things like that. Um, so it's affected us all like that.'

Fathers sometimes find it harder to cope than mothers:

'As far as he was concerned it was his child and there was nothing wrong with his children, sort of thing, and he just wouldn't accept it anyway.'

Family activities can be disrupted:

'Just that it's terrible and it like ruins your life. It ruins our life. That sounds selfish, but it does. You know like, you're wanting to go out somewhere and we're all ready, and Tracey has a seizure. So you can't go for like an hour, an hour and a half afterwards. And we wanted to take her to watch 'Disney on Ice', but like I said, it's going to sound really bad, but it's a waste of money. If she goes and has a seizure in the middle of it, and we have to come home, what's the point in going?'

Sometimes all that is needed is reassurance. This comes best from clear, simple information about the effects and implications. And honesty:

'They kept telling us that he would grow out of it, because nocturnal epilepsy, they expected him to grow out of it. Well, he's 19, he still hasn't, and I don't suppose that he will now. I don't know why they give you that false hope, and then it's broken.'

43

Epilepsy

Generalized information that does not focus on this child and their family is next to useless. It cannot be said firmly enough that the only effective way in which parents and professionals can work together is on an *informal* basis. They can then share valuable information without fear of repercussions. We are reminded of the adage, 'no victims, no heroes'. Life with epilepsy can, and indeed must, go on. The new legislation and codes of practice will facilitate this. It's up to all to be vigilant, and for professionals to listen and learn.

References

Johnson, M. C. and L. Thomas (1998) *The Code of Practice on the Identification and Assessment of Special Needs (SEN) and Pupils with an Epileptic Condition.* Manchester, Manchester Metropolitan University (unpublished).

3 What Next?

Keeping the child involved

Throughout this book we emphasize that epilepsy is not an illness of which you can be cured. It is a medical condition (because it requires the attention of doctors) with which you live. The emphasis is on the last word in that sentence – live. From our survey it became clear how vital it was not to let the condition take over either the child or (worse) the whole family. There are other conditions to which this applies, asthma and migraine being the two most obvious. Knowledge and understanding are the keys to maintaining control of life with epilepsy. However, one's own knowledge and understanding are only the start. Generating knowledge and understanding in others is the second step.

Language has an important role to play. What you have is a family member with epilepsy, not an epileptic in the family. When talking to heads and teachers in schools we were struck by their unnecessary use of medical terminology. Pupils couldn't just 'take their pills', 'medication' had to be 'administered'. So, just as children have routinely to wash, brush their teeth and comb their hair, children with epilepsy have also to take their pills. When they are out on the streets they need to be aware of traffic and other people. They need to be able to recognize when they feel vulnerable. They need to know what signals possible danger. Equally they need to be aware of the signs of an incipient seizure – 'aura', and what to do about it. It's all really just an extension of 'street-cred'. The crucial thing is to recognize the child's age and level of maturity. Don't expect them to be able to handle things below their maturity level but insist that they do handle those that are. The only person who will always be there is them!

DfES, *Managing Medicines in Schools and Early Years Settings* (2005), para. 45 says:

> It is good practice to encourage children, who are able, to take responsibility to manage their own medicines from a relatively early age and schools should encourage this.

Access to the curriculum – a whole-school approach

The main area where, having sorted out their family dynamics parents will have to be vigilant on their child's behalf is at school. The family now has a *child* with epilepsy; the school now has a *pupil* with epilepsy. Both must focus on the word in italics. Since Johnson and Thomas (1999) did their survey the regulations relating to pupils with medical conditions and/or SEN have been strengthened and clarified. The medical guidance document that was available then, *Supporting Pupils with Medical Needs: A good practice guide* (DoH, 1996) has been superseded by *Managing Medicines in Schools and Early Years Settings* (DfES, 2005) (http://publications. teachernet.gov.uk/managing + medicines + in + schools). In addition there is now the protection of the SEN and Disability Act 2001 and the recent Disability Discrimination Act 2005 (available at: www.drc-gb.org/thelaw/ thedda.asp). For those wanting a fuller analysis of the current medical position than we give here there is the National Institute for Clinical Excellence, 'Clinical Guideline 20: The Epilepsies' (NICE, 2004) (www.nice.org.uk/ CGO20NICEguideline).

These documents back up the fundamental national curriculum statement that all children, whatever their disability or difficulties, are to have access to a range of core subjects. Teaching methods may need to be adjusted to allow for the pupil's *style* of learning and also to support the management of his or her epilepsy within the school environment. Joining in with physical activities, such as field or school trips and outings, is also included. However, we must recognize that staff may be concerned about health and safety related issues reinforced by worries about litigation. Often, exclusion rather than inclusion seems the easiest, cheapest and safest answer. Nevertheless, schools are obliged to include children with epilepsy in all aspects of the national curriculum. A national curriculum document (DfEE, 1999) states clearly the three principles of Inclusion:

Epilepsy

- setting suitable learning challenges;
- responding to pupils' diverse learning needs;
- overcoming potential barriers to learning and assessment for individuals and groups of pupils.

Teachers' fears can be reduced if they know:

- what to expect
- what to do
- who to notify
- how to cope,

along with receiving professional development relating to:

- how to organize the environment
- appropriate teaching and emotional requirements
- level of risk
- realistic expectations of the child's overall potential and day-to-day learning.

Many children with epilepsy suffer a sense of frustration and/or low self-esteem because of their epilepsy. Teachers can actively seek to improve the child's view of him/herself both as an individual and in relation to his or her peers, by organizing their lessons to encourage mutual cooperation and support rather than competition and individual achievement. This may be achieved in a variety of ways.

All staff should be encouraged to have an attitude of:

- positive promotion of attitudes towards students with disabilities – particularly those with 'hidden' or 'unseen' disabilities which can sometimes be harder for peers to accept;
- encouragement of an atmosphere which nurtures high expectations, high-quality planning and (where needed) professional support on an individual basis;
- encouragement (and allowance for) reasonable risk-taking within specified subject/activity areas.

Academic subjects

When planning for either the whole class or an individual, the following principles may be useful.

Students with epilepsy need clear routines and structures when being presented with information. Remember that epilepsy can affect the following:

- taking in information, especially if this is presented in large chunks
- retaining, processing, categorizing and prioritizing that information
- formulating and expressing an answer either verbally or in writing.

Teachers can help by:

- presenting information in short chunks
- reinforcing verbal information with written notes or bullet-pointed handouts

- providing direct support when the pupil is felt to have difficulty in maintaining a focus of attention – particularly when working in group settings.

Schools set homework at both primary and secondary school level. Coursework requirements for GCSEs, NVQ units and, in a more academically formal way, for A- and AS-level can lead to a heavy overall workload. This should be kept under review.

Epilepsy can have a marked effect on:

- attention control
- short-term memory (usually temporary in this context)
- self-composure
- mood
- behaviour
- tolerance of light and ambient noise.

Key Stage tests and formal examination arrangements

The Joint Council of the Examination Boards provides advice on special arrangements for children with various conditions and disabilities. It gives specific guidance for children with hearing and visual impairments, learning disabilities and dyslexia. There are also guidelines for those under SEN provision. Arrangements include:

- extra time (usually on a ratio per hour basis)

- rest breaks
- stopping times (similar to rest breaks but can be unscheduled).

Examinations and assessed work

Many children with epilepsy have attention-control problems and find it difficult to focus on test and examination work for more than short periods of time. Others may be at increased risk of having seizures in stressful situations. Some pupils may be prone to having seizures at certain times of day which can be allowed for within the standard school timetable but not when formal examinations are in progress. For such children it is often advisable to arrange for the test or examination to be taken in a separate room or away from the school. In such cases it might be helpful for the pupil to sit the examination in their own home, another institution – maybe a smaller unit attached to another school – or in hospital if the child is unwell. There is no need to seek permission provided that:

- the test takes place according to the timetable laid down by the statutory authority;
- although the examination time may be interrupted for 'rest breaks', the total time allowed remains the same as under normal circumstances;
- security and confidentiality of material is adhered to;
- the invigilator is not a relative of the candidate.

Epilepsy

Emergency permission may need to be sought if the pupil has a seizure unexpectedly within the period of the examination or within a period of time, e.g. 12 hours prior to the examination when it is felt that the pupil's performance would be adversely affected to a significant degree. The headteacher is responsible for notifying the LEA or Examining Board of any emergency arrangements required.

The Joint Council for General Qualifications recognizes that:

> there are some candidates who have coped with the learning demands of a course, but for whom the standard arrangements for the assessment of their attainment may present a barrier. This applies both in the case of candidates with known and long-standing learning problems and candidates who are affected at or near the time of assessment. Such barriers may arise as a result of:
>
> - 2.1 a permanent or long-term disability or learning difficulty
> - 2.2 a temporary illness, disability or indisposition
> - 2.3 the immediate circumstances of the assessment.
>
> (Introduction to Regulations and Guidance, 2002, p. 2)

See Appendix for details of how to download updates on access arrangements.

Practical subjects and laboratory-based work

Schools are naturally anxious about placing a student whom they feel to be 'at risk' of injury in a vulnerable or dangerous situation, particularly if they:

- are known to experience seizures without warning;
- have atonic or 'drop attacks' which are known to occur suddenly and can cause head, facial or other injury;
- will be handling dangerous substances, e.g. inflammable or corrosive liquids or equipment where they might be burnt.

The Five Guiding Principles as set out by the Qualifications and Curriculum Authority (QCA) Paper 'Including all Learners':

i.   the inclusion of all learners at relevant levels of activity
ii. opportunities for continuity and progression for all learners
iii. achievement of the highest possible standards for all learners
iv. the recognition of achievement of all learners
v.   the provision of easily accessible advice and guidance for all learners.

In making a decision they should take into account:

- the likelihood of a seizure occurring (many seizures only happen at certain times of the day, week or month);

- the type of seizure that is most expected;
- whether the person is at risk of losing consciousness or experiencing impaired awareness of the surroundings, and for how long;
- the level of supervision required to meet the perceived risk.

PE/outdoor pursuits and swimming

Climbing, abseiling and similar activities involving height can cause teachers to worry. It is also a commonly held view that children with epilepsy are not advised to go swimming. Providing proper precautions are taken there are no reasons why a child with epilepsy may not go swimming, although scuba-diving, jet-skiing and similar activities may not be a good idea.

A 'buddy' system, where one of a child's friends stays by the child throughout the time of the activity, can help. Don't overprotect a child with epilepsy or single them out as someone special or different. They should be encouraged to join in as many activities as possible.

However, pool staff should be alert to a swimmer:

- making inappropriate or unexpected changes of direction
- not responding to their name when called
- becoming uncoordinated or ceasing to swim
- jerking or stiffening involuntarily their arms, legs or head
- crying out.

They should have training on what to do if they see any of these signs.

How do parents ensure that their child is treated appropriately by the school?

The first thing to recognize is that schools are awash with documentation, all of it in the 'public domain'. Probably the best first step is to look at the school's latest Ofsted report. This is on the web at www.ofsted.gov.uk. This will tell you whether the inspectors thought the school's policies and practices towards pupils who have 'different' needs are good and sympathetic. You then need to ask for copies of the school's policy documents for pupils with SEN. This doesn't mean that your child will necessarily have special needs, but the document will show you how the school approaches pupils on an individual level. In particular you should look to see if it mentions epilepsy. Our survey showed that the best professional development in this area is experience. Teachers who had previously taught a pupil with epilepsy were far more effective in dealing with others. Look also at the list of staff to see if there is a school nurse, preferably one with qualifications in or experience of epilepsy.

DfES (2005) para. 13 states, 'Parents have the prime responsibility for their child's health and should provide schools and settings with information about their child's medical condition'. So you now need to ask for an appointment with the head, the SENCO and the nurse if one is available. Be clear about what the consultant and the GP have said and, particularly, how you have found it most effective to meet your child's needs at home. If you have written notes about all this – so much the better. Also be clear about what your child thinks they need in order to be able to do their best. Modern practice suggests that, if possible, the pupil should also be involved in the meeting. However, if there is resistance to this from the school it would be better to have a meeting without them rather that one that gets off on the 'wrong foot'.

DfES (2005) makes it clear that, 'Children with medical needs have the same rights of admission to a school setting as other children' (p. 4, para. 4). They should also be protected under the DDA 1995, as epilepsy is a 'Physical or mental impairment which has a substantial and long-term effect on his (or her) abilities to carry out normal day-to-day tasks'. It also states that early years settings are under the same obligations. Many modern drugs need only be taken twice a day so having them in school may not be the issue it was when our survey was done. 'Schools should consider the issue of managing administration of medicines', but 'there is no legal duty on staff to administer medicines'. However, they 'should ensure that they have sufficient members of support staff who are appropriately trained to manage medicines as part of their duties' (paras 15 and 16). This may mean that if your child has to be on a 'three-times-a-day' routine, support staff will look after the drugs but the child administers them. Form 7 attached to DfES (2005) is a suggested parental consent form. Forms 3a and b are useful for parents to record details of medicines their child is taking. Form 4 is to confirm that a member of staff will give the child the medicine. Whilst not a requirement, it is useful for the school to keep a record of all medicines administered. Forms 5 and 6 provide good examples of record forms.

What schools must have is a policy, 'to enable regular attendance. Formal systems and procedures in respect of administering medicines, developed in partnership with parents and staff, should back up this policy' (para. 22). The contents of that policy should include:

- procedures for managing prescription medicines that need to be taken during the school day
- procedures for managing prescription medicines on school trips and outings
- clear statement on the roles and responsibilities of staff
- clear statement of parental responsibilities
- need for prior agreement from parents for any medicines to be given to the child
- circumstances in which children may take non-prescription medicines
- school policy on assisting children with medical needs
- policy on children carrying medicines themselves
- staff training in dealing with medical needs
- record keeping
- safe storage of medicines
- access to school's emergency procedures
- risk assessment and management procedures.

This last point is very important. Under the DDA a child cannot be excluded from any activity unless the special arrangements that would have to be made to include them are 'unreasonable'. Before this can be claimed a risk assessment must take place. This is a formal procedure, not just the decision of the 'management'.

A risk assessment is a careful examination of what might cause harm to those involved in a particular situation so that precautions can be put in place to prevent that harm occurring. As well as physical or mental harm it must consider harm to the pupil's education.

The important things to consider are whether the feature it is believed may cause the harm is *significant* and whether the risk it poses is small or large. It must also consider whether that risk is already covered by reasonable adjustments. Only when it can be shown that there is no alternative should refusal to allow a pupil to take part in an activity be considered.

How are the risks to be assessed?

There are five steps to be taken and documented by school staff:

1. Seek and/or list the suspected sources of risk.
2. Decide who might be harmed, how and to what extent.
3. Evaluate each risk and decide whether existing reasonable adjustments are adequate or whether more needs to be done.
4. Record the findings.
5. Review the assessments, revisit if necessary and, if any new adjustments are needed, decide if they are 'reasonable and if so implement them.

Step 1 – Detail the risks

Any person who has raised the issue of potential risk should state clearly in writing what they believe that risk to be. If the process is to go further, that potential risk must be *significant* and likely to result in serious harm or affect several people. (This is similar to the DDA requirement that a disability must be serious and permanent.)

Step 2 – Decide who might be harmed and how

This will include pupils, teachers, assistants and other staff.

Step 3 – Evaluate the risks in relation to those identified in Step 2

Each risk should be considered. It is not enough to feel or think that the people identified might be affected adversely but there must be evidence that the problems are starting to occur or have occurred consistently. The important thing to have is evidence. It is unlikely that any risks can be reduced to zero. The aim is to be clear whether the remaining risk, after amendments have been made, is high, medium or low.

Step 4 – Record the findings

This is the only way that the extent and nature of the potential harm can become clear to all. The document needs to show that:

- a careful check was made to state clearly and fully the nature of the hazard;
- all those potentially or actually affected by it were consulted;
- the risks to all the relevant people were considered and quantified;
- the arrangements proposed to minimise the hazard(s) were considered.

Step 5 – Arrive at, record and disseminate the decision

If the risk can be reduced to low by amendments to the reasonable adjustments, an action plan should be drawn up and implemented.

Even if taking the pills is not an issue, the side-effects of them as well as the effects of the epilepsy itself must be discussed, and arrangements to minimize them agreed. Para. 38 states:

If the child's medical needs are inadequately supported this may have a significant impact on a child's experiences and the way they function. The impact may be direct in that it may affect cognitive or physical abilities, behaviour or emotional state. Some medicines may also affect learning leading to poor concentration or difficulties in remembering. [However,] It is the child's educational needs rather than the medical diagnosis that *must* [original emphasis] be considered.

Our survey revealed some very poor practice in this regard. Firstly it was very clear that staff must not rely on the hospital or the GP to pass information to the school. Consultants admit that the flow of information is not as effective as it should be and in some cases the system breaks down and the information never reaches the school.

'When we see a child at clinic, we send a copy to the community paediatrician who oversees a number of school doctors, who each oversee one or two schools. It's like sort of feeding it down and now and then it's like Chinese Whispers, and you can imagine, letters often get lost, somewhere in the community paediatric path, and never get down to the school doctor.'

At the first meeting parents should find out who is supposed to be the channel for information to and from the school, but don't rely on it working effectively. There needs to be a continual flow of information between all those involved with the child, achievable only by talking to one another. Every contact, for whatever reason, should be seen as an opportunity for developing understanding. In our survey one parent told us:

'But it's like banging your head on a brick wall. I mean I can't, I wouldn't like to count the number of times I've been to this school, you know, to try and get extra help for her and to explain the problems yet again, to another teacher, who then tells me she will tell everybody else who is involved, and doesn't.'

Epilepsy

Be particularly cautious if you are asked just to fill in a form. Experiences that parents recounted suggest that questionnaires they completed at the start of school ask general questions about their child's condition. Specific questions were not asked about how the condition manifests itself in their particular child – this information being vitally important for any class teacher. There is also a tendency for forms to be filed away and the information not disseminated to those who need to know. Again, what you may feel appropriate to write on a form may be far less than you would say if talking informally to a member of staff face to face, or even perhaps within a group.

It is only when schools actually experience having a child with epilepsy that it becomes a way of life for the staff. One way that teachers might get this experience, albeit artificial, could be through epilepsy workshops. However, this must be done 'for real'. They need to have a pupil in mind, preferably with the parents present, to make it part of their 'active knowledge'. This would be of far greater value than all the pre-admission questionnaires.

If you have been introduced to a Sapphire Nurse by the hospital or GP they could be invaluable at such a meeting. If you haven't met one already you can contact the Epilepsy Action helpline for full details of your local Sapphire Nurse service on 0808 800 5050. Annex D to DfES (2005) lists contact details of other voluntary organizations able to provide advice or packs advising staff on how to support children with medical needs.

'They did phone quite often with every slight thing, but again I think when the Sapphire Nurse had a word with them, I think they relaxed more, that I didn't have to be called if he'd fallen over,' one parent told us.

Experience of dealing with a number of schools indicates that teachers and, sadly, members of the School Health Service still view epilepsy as a simple construct of major and minor seizures, with very little knowledge about its many differing forms, both clinical and sub-clinical, which may be constraining the growth of learning and behaviour in children (Scrambler, 1990). This issue was also talked about by one of the specialist epilepsy nurses, as she explained:

'Very often schools see a child who has absence seizures. You know, they think, there's no problem here, because the seizures aren't dead dramatic, there's no problem and yet they're not aware that, you know, the child is totally unconscious at this point, therefore there is a problem that needs to be looked at and monitored. Some schools see it not as a problem at all.'

Comments parents made support this:

'Well, I don't think they realize that there's all forms of epilepsy. They just put it down to . . . they just thought she'd be thrashing around on the floor, or something, sort of thing, they don't realize that there are absences and things like that. They're very naive.'

Even after explaining to the school about her daughter's absences, this parent felt that the school had no understanding about the condition, which she found very frustrating:

'Her teacher said she wouldn't be so bad if she didn't daydream quite so much, you know, if she paid more attention she'd get more out of it. And I'd say, "Well do you not think perhaps that this is, you know, the epilepsy?". And she said, "Oh, I don't think so dear, we would have noticed that." This is the attitude we used to have. And I'd say, "But that is how it manifests itself, you know". Oh, you know, I was so exasperated I just couldn't get through.'

Another told of an incident that clearly shows that the school had no understanding about the condition at all, an incident that must border on child abuse:

'. . . Yes, she's had two lots of detention because she had fits at school, one in the playground at school. Her teacher gave her a red card because she was slumped up against a wall, and when the whistle was blown, she didn't respond. And because she didn't respond for two minutes the teacher left her, she got everyone into line, and because she still hadn't responded she gave her a red card. And she started shouting at her and of course she eventually started coming out of the fit, and couldn't understand why everyone was shouting at her, and just went hysterical.'

These comments suggest that when seizures are not dramatic then the fact that the child has epilepsy goes out of teachers' consciousness. The most difficult form of epilepsy for schools to come to terms with is petit-mal or absence seizures. As we have shown earlier this may lead to unawareness of surroundings for perhaps just seconds. The problem is that this can look, to teachers, like daydreaming. The results for child and parent can be most frustrating.

'She'd been at this school for three weeks and I said, you know, "How's she doing with the fits, are you noticing many?", because I was a bit concerned . . . And her teacher said, "What do you mean, fits?", and I said, "Well, she has epilepsy." And she said, "Oh, I didn't know." So then I had a meeting with her and we went into it in great detail, what happens, and she said, "Oh, I wondered why she didn't answer me."'

Fortunately it wasn't always like that:

'When he was diagnosed, he was at Junior School, when he changed to the new school, they said it was absence, this other girl who I spoke to said the teachers were all aware of it and er, they, you know, they knew they'd to keep an eye on him . . . and if they thought that he'd missed anything in lesson, they would go over it with him.'

Epilepsy

Some staff were aware of the possible side-effects of medication whilst others did not seem to be. Understanding ranged from the superficial:

'I can only speak from the one child that I've taught and I was very aware that the medication could make him sleepy and that at times he would not respond as, um, quickly, as he, I would expect, but it didn't really seem to be a big problem.'

to the quite sophisticated:

'Well I suppose there's two aspects to that. There's the actual medical condition, which may be the epilepsy and the effect that that would have, you know, whether he was having petit mals and was blanking off and wasn't, if you like, wasn't receiving that day, or that period of time, because I believe it's a short period of time, isn't it, you know. And it could be the effects of the drugs as well. So there are two sides to that.'

It is essential that staff are aware of the possible side-effects of medication, in terms of both educational implications and possible changes in the child's behaviour, so that the change in the child is not misinterpreted as being something else, i.e. being lazy. Information should be aimed at demystification. We are not talking about hard drug', just pills that a child has to learn to take to control his or her condition in the same way that they need to learn to brush their teeth or not forget their glasses.

When school staff first meet it, epilepsy can be both frightening and frustrating.

'You know, you feel like, OK you've been told something and certain information, but you think well, should I know more? You know, you feel a little bit in the dark and it's a bit of a worry, you know, if someone's going to have a fit in the classroom, or they're going to have, you know, something's going to happen, or suddenly an asthma attack.'

'Well I mean I asked his mum what we should do, and sort of spoke to her a few times, and when he sort of didn't have any, it became a lot easier. But it was still the fear of not knowing what to expect that worried us.'

But once staff have survived the first experience:

'It's certainly been a learning process for us, I think, which we have gone through and I think that it has raised our level of awareness, in terms of possible future pupils.'

'It's like you learn as you go along. I mean until Wayne I hadn't taught anyone with it before. If it happened again I think that I would be more relaxed about being able to cope with it.'

Parents really can help:

'We didn't realize at even the outset, we did not realize, you know how much we needed to learn about the condition. I mean we knew the basics but with mum's help we learnt to deal with it, and knew what to expect.'

And boys will be boys:

'We learned to distinguish between a real fit and a pseudo-fit. Because, as most teenagers, he clicked, "If I don't want to do that, if I have a fit, I'm out of it." So he was having quite a few.'

In the survey, schools felt in two minds about parents' wishes:

'Thinking about the individual cases in the school, it probably would depend on the parents' wishes. And the student. That has happened on one occasion, I know, when both the child and the parents wanted her to stay in school, and she did. I think, generally, that we would insist that they went home.'

'It would be more than likely that parents would be contacted straight away and they would be taken home.'

However, some of the comments that parents made suggest that they did not want their child to be sent home after they had had a seizure.

'If she was bad, then they'd ring for us to pick her up, which was okay, but sometimes I thought that maybe it would have been better had she slept at school and then she could have gone back into class and carried on.'

'They dealt with it, but they wanted me to come and take him home. But, it, it would be nicer if they would allow him to sleep it off in the medical room, but I think, I don't know whether they feel they're vulnerable that way, or what, I'm not sure.'

'He usually sleeps in the classroom because they haven't got a medical room. So he sleeps in the quiet corner and then joins the class again after about 15, 20 minutes.'

There can be real practical difficulties of always being expected to pick the child up from school when s/he has had a seizure.

One of the specialist epilepsy nurses also commented:

'The parents don't even feel that they can go shopping, they have to be by the phone at all times. I have tried to address this with the schools that perhaps all the child needs is to sleep in a corner of the classroom to recover. But, it's a major problem for some families. I've not found the ideal solution really for this.'

From the comments made above, one can see a discrepancy between schools' perceptions that they are doing what parents want, and what the parents actually do want. The act of sending the child home after he has a seizure once again suggests that schools perceive the child as being ill, consequently they should not be in school, rather than seeing the child as having a condition and the seizure being a symptom of that condition.

As we said earlier, the pupil and their parents are the only ones who have that particular child's needs at the front of their minds. Teachers and other professionals have, rightly, many others to consider. It is vital, there-fore, for parents to keep track of what is happening (or not) at school; at the same time remembering that dilemmas can easily arise because of the needs of others. The best way is just to have a keen interest in your child's progress. Be aware when staff try to get away by talking in very general terms. Things we are interested in we talk about in detail. Things we want to avoid are skated over. If you become concerned it may be well to follow the advice in para. 40:

'It is often helpful to develop a written health care plan, involving the parents and relevant health professionals.'

(DfES 2005)

The healthcare plan can include:

- details of the child's condition
- special requirements
- side-effects of medicines
- what constitutes an emergency
- what action to take in an emergency

- what not to do in an emergency
- who to contact in an emergency
- the role that staff can play.

Form 2, available with DfES (2005) gives an example.

Asking for such a plan will give a good signal to the school that you know what you are talking about and also give you a document to fall back on if problems arise.

Comments most of the parents made suggest that they would like to work collaboratively with staff to gain information about medical and educational developments with their child. However, it seems that the school does not always reciprocate:

'He was having a few [seizures], we asked at the school if they'd keep a record for us because they saw him more through the day, so that we could tell, but they never bothered.'

This parent talked about a similar experience. Due to a change in medication, she wanted to know if there should be any changes in order to monitor and record developments:

'And she was falling asleep in the playground or at her desk, or things like that. They would just leave her. They wouldn't tell me they'd been happening or anything, other children would tell me these things had been happening. You know, when we had them back for tea, and things like this. And then I'd go in and ask and the teacher would say, ''No, she's been the same as usual really,'' because I needed to know, because at that time they were still trying to adjust the medication. It was obviously affecting her entire life and I needed to know these things.'

In contrast, some parents felt that schools were very cooperative and more than willing to pass on information:

'The school were very good, you know, when she had time off and things like that. If she had been ill in the night I could go into school and ask the class teacher what they had been doing so that I could help her to catch up with the work, and Mrs D. would be more than willing to tell me what they had been up to, you know.'

Some parents felt that the school was very good with their child and talked positively about their experiences:

'I've got an absolutely brilliant class teacher at the moment, he is brilliant. Um, in this class they're now going to start going swimming, and I was terrified because obviously she's got to have a one-to-one watcher. And, um, I went in to see him about it, and we – my husband was there – and he said, ''It's all right, it's already organized.'' So there's no problem there. So we're just waiting now for them to actually start swimming.'

'The staff from school were lovely about it. They rang home about it, and the, some of the children had been quite upset, obviously, to see her having a fit and, um, the year tutor, just sat them all down and said, "Look this is it. You've got to be nice with Brenda."'

'They were fine, yes. The first teacher she had there was brilliant, she asked me if I could take a little picture of Alice in so that they could put it on the staff-room notice board, so that the other teachers would recognize her, which I think was very nice. That was reassuring. Um, when Alice went into the Juniors, that would be her second teacher, um, they rang me up about the swimming, you know, to check that I had no problem with her going swimming.'

This raises the issue of confidentiality. Most import-antly it raises the issue of other pupils' reactions. Clearly if schools and classes were cooperative, mutually suppor-tive communities then openness would be appropriate. However, without becoming enmeshed in the 'edu-politics' of streaming, setting and the merits of competi-tion and individual attainment, parents would be well advised to look at what Ofsted have said in regard to the 'emotional climate' and pastoral care in the school. They should also be alert to any signs of lowered self-esteem in their child and react to this earlier rather than later.

We encountered many good reports:

'I've never really met any negative attitudes. Most of the teachers have been pretty good. Most of them have obviously said, "What are we to expect?", and luckily, when she went into junior school, even though we'd moved to a different area, one of the supply teachers who'd been at her infant school was then in the junior school, and she suffered from fits herself. And Jen found that she could go and talk to her to find out more, you know. Because she's never really known anybody else, apart from that one teacher, who's actually had fits.'

'Excellent. They forget it – it sounds awful that. But they don't forget because they know it's there, and that's that.'

As with the doctors and hospitals, schools need to recognize that when dealing with a pupil who has epilepsy they are dealing with the pupil and not the epilepsy. Their full inclusion in the class and school should not be a problem. The parent usually has all the information they will need about the condition, its effects and how to deal with them. All the strategies our parents reported from schools they were satisfied with are just simple, thoughtful responses to an individual child's needs. Fear and prejudice are the barriers. Openness, personal and mutual regard are the attitudes that engender successful partnerships.

We have made extensive use of the forms and procedures in DfES (2005). We do not want to imply that there is a need for such formality in every case. The comments from the survey parents show clearly that it is *informal* contacts that work best. However, we do feel that DfES (2005) provides a very firm back-up for parents who feel that their child's needs are not being taken seriously. If you are not confident that the school is acting in the child's best interest, merely indicating that you know that the document exists may well be enough to get action. The next step is to formally request that one or other of the plans be initiated. If the child is being excluded from any part of the curriculum or activities then certainly insist on a Risk Assessment. If this is refused, go straight to DDA procedures. One thing we would certainly advise all parents to do is to start a log or diary as soon as the GP refers your child to the hospital. Make written notes at all consultations or you will forget what has been said. Keep in the log all letters, etc. that you are sent or write. If you use the phone, make a note of the date and time, the name of the person you spoke to and a digest of what was said and/or agreed. You may not need it, but in our experience there are only two sorts of parents in this regard – those who did keep such a record and those who wish they had! If nothing else you will have a great sense of relief when you are able to burn the lot if all has gone well.

So far we have assumed that with understanding and sympathetic cooperation, the majority of children and young people with epilepsy will achieve successfully in a mainstream school. However, there are those who do not. This may be either because they have additional difficulties or the effects of the epilepsy and/or their medication are severe or because the level of support offered is insufficient. In these cases the Special Educational Needs Code of Practice (DfES, 2001) comes into play. This replaces the original 1994 document. The

Epilepsy

DfES has written a guide to SEN for parents and carers. It introduces it by saying:

> This guide aims to help you understand:
> - what special educational needs are;
> - what you can do if you are worried that your child may be having difficulties before they go to school;
> - how you can help your child;
> - what early education settings and schools can do to help your child;
> - what local education authorities and other services can do to help your child;
> - your rights and your child's rights.
>
> You can get a copy from the DfES at www.teacher-net.gov.uk/wholeschool/sen.

It goes on to say:

> The term 'special educational needs' has a legal definition. Children with special educational needs all have learning difficulties or disabilities that make it harder for them to learn than most children of the same age. These children may need extra or different help from that given to other children of the same age.
>
> Children with special educational needs may need extra help because of a range of needs, such as thinking and understanding, physical or sensory difficulties, emotional and behavioural difficulties, or difficulties with speech and language or how they relate to and behave with other people.

Many children will have special educational needs of some kind at some time during their education. Schools and other organisations can help most children overcome the barriers their difficulties present quickly and easily. But a few children will need extra help for some or all of their time in school.

So SEN could mean that a child has difficulty with:

- all the work in school
- reading, writing, number work or understanding information
- expressing themselves or understanding what others are saying
- making friends or relating to adults
- behaving properly in school
- organizing themselves
- their sensory or physical support needs which may affect them in school.

As you can see many of these may, but need not necessarily, apply to children with epilepsy.

A very valuable source of further information can be found on the website of 'Inclusive Technology' at www.inclusive.co.uk/infosite/code.shtml.

The 1994 Code outlined a five-stage approach to identification and assessment. The revised Code replaced this with a graduated, three-stage approach:

- early years/school action
- early years/school action plus
- statemented provision.

Epilepsy

The eight areas of SEN identified in the original code have been replaced by four key areas of SEN:

1. Communication and interaction
2. Cognition and learning
3. Behaviour, emotional and social development
4. Sensory and/or physical needs.

Support given to a pupil under the Code will normally be in the form of an Individual Education Plan (IEP), focusing on what is additional to and different from the rest of the curriculum provided by the school. This is known as 'School Action'. In early years settings it is known as Early Years Action. If there has been Early Years Action, the primary school is expected to carry on whatever support has been agreed in a manner appropriate to that school. Where external agencies such as speech and language therapy or educational psychology are involved, the support may then be known as School Action Plus or Early Years Action Plus.

The school is required to provide learning opportunities for all pupils conforming to the three key principles for inclusion in the National Curriculum Statement (QCA, 1999):

1. Setting suitable learning challenges
2. Responding to pupils' diverse needs
3. Overcoming potential barriers to learning and assessment for individuals and groups of pupils.

When a class teacher or a SENCO thinks that a child may not be making adequate progress, they must first and foremost inform the parents. 'Adequate progress' may be progress which:

- Closes the attainment gap between the child and their peers
- Prevents the attainment gap getting any wider
- Is similar to that of peers starting from the same attainment baseline, but less than the majority of their peers
- Matches or betters the child's previous rate of progress
- Ensures access to the full curriculum
- Demonstrates an improvement in self-help, social or personal skills
- Demonstrates improvements in the child's behaviour.

The Code gives five triggers for School Action intervention. These must be underpinned with evidence and relate to a child who, despite receiving differentiated learning opportunities:

1. makes little or no progress even when teaching approaches are targeted particularly on a child's identified area of weakness
2. shows signs of difficulty in developing literacy or mathematics skills which result in poor attainment in some curriculum areas
3. presents persistent emotional or behavioural difficulties which are not ameliorated by the behaviour-management techniques usually employed in the school

4. has sensory or physical problems, and continues to make little or no progress despite the provision of specialist equipment
5. has communication and/or interaction difficulties, and continues to make little or no progress despite the provision of a differentiated curriculum.

If the class teacher, in consultation with the parents, feels the child needs further support than the school normally gives, they will call a meeting with the school SENCO who may also get further information from any relevant professionals with the agreement of the parents. Ultimately an agreement is reached on the action needed to help the child progress. This *may* involve extra staff and or one-to-one tuition in some area/s, but not necessarily. It may be different teaching materials, group or individual support. For instance, in the case of a child with absence seizures it may involve extra time at the end of a session to make sure nothing has been missed. For a child with tonic-clonic seizures it may mean extra time to go over what was missed as a result of the seizure. Equally, it may mean some professional development for the staff in relation to the child's particular needs. Whatever is decided will be recorded in an IEP. This will include information about:

- the short-term targets for the child
- the teaching strategies to be used
- the provision to be put in place
- when the plan is to be renewed
- success and/or exit criteria
- outcomes (to be recorded when the IEP is reviewed).

If, despite receiving support under School Action, progress is still not satisfactory, the external support agencies can be involved under School Action Plus. Again, there are triggers for this and the parents (and child) must be fully involved in all discussions and decisions.

If after School Action and School Action Plus progress is still not satisfactory, either the school or the parent can ask for a Statutory Assessment with a view to getting a Statement for the child. These are dealt with in Chapters 7 and 8 of the Code, and the LEA and/or the school should put parents in touch with the Parent Partnership Adviser to help them through the process. Good independent sources of information are:

http://inclusion.uwe.ac.uk/csie/ukedlaw.htm
www.bbc.co.uk/schools/parents/life/sen/statements/
www.bbc.co.uk/schools/parents/life/sen/statements/
   sen_statementproblems.shtml
www.parentscentre.gov.uk/specialneeds/
   specialeducationalneeds

There are also useful critiques at:

www.ipsea.org.uk/

However, let us emphasize again – you should not assume that a child will have SEN merely because they have epilepsy.

References

Scrambler, G. (1990) 'Social factors and quality of care in epilepsy', in *Quality of Life and Quality of Care in Epilepsy.* London, Royal Society of Medicine.

4 Management of Epilepsy in Schools

> When talking to parents about their child, schools need to stop talking in general or quasi-medical terms about the epilepsy and focus on the individual child and asks how the condition manifests itself in that particular child and what both they and the child can do about it . . . staff are then able . . . to create a learning and emotional environment that best meets the needs of the child.
>
> (Johnson and Thomas, 1998)

Research from as far back as the 1950s stresses the increased risk of children with medical conditions, including epilepsy, underachieving at school. Clearly this can be for a number of reasons. The impact of the condition may be lessened if the implications of epilepsy and seizure management are appreciated and understood by staff, and appropriate policy and practice are in place to support any actions which need to be taken regarding the child's care and well-being while he or she is in school.

Children should be central to school thinking about epilepsy. We should be planning so the school environment meets their needs and allows them the same freedom of choice as their peers, rather than trying to make them fit into rigid and often ill-informed policy and guidance that has, for example with the recent introduction of *Managing Medicines in Schools and Early Years Settings* (DfES 2005), changed how emergency (rescue) medication may be given to children who have seizures while they are at school.

Though this chapter provides staff with fairly comprehensive information about seizure management and the management of medicines in schools, we recommend that for further information you call the Epilepsy Action's helpline on 0800 800 5050 or go to their website www.epilepsy.org.uk for more detailed information.

First aid for seizures

Do not move the child, unless they are in danger of coming into contact with potentially dangerous objects that are hard, pointed or likely to burn them, for instance.

Place something soft under the child's head – an item of clothing, exercise mat or firm pillow or cushion.

Stay with the child or make sure someone s/he knows does, until s/he regains consciousness. They may be frightened and or confused when they come round so it is important that someone is there when this happens. This is particularly important following a myoclonic, absence or complex partial seizure when the child may only have lost consciousness fleetingly or retained some awareness while the seizure was in progress.

Stay quietly and calmly with them. Reassure them but do not overwhelm them. Give information on what has happened on a 'need to know' basis to begin with.

Only call an ambulance if:

- There is no record of the child ever having had a seizure.
- The seizure lasts for more than five minutes.
- One seizure follows another (usually tonic-clonic) without the child recovering or regaining consciousness between them.
- The child sustains an injury following a seizure. (This is particularly likely to happen in association with an atonic seizure when the child has fallen suddenly to the ground without being able to save him/herself.)
- You feel the child is otherwise in urgent need of medical attention.

Children with regular atonic seizures may need to wear protective headgear such as a cycle helmet or similar, in order to lessen the risk of repeated injury, especially to the face.

During a complex partial seizure the child may appear to be distracted and unresponsive to what is being said to them. They may display repeated movements such as swallowing, chewing, lip smacking, scratching or hitting themselves. They may also have no recollection of what immediately preceded or took place during the seizure, even though their eyes may be open. Do not restrain the child unless they are in immediate danger. When it is over, reassurance is very important as the child will feel disorientated and possibly upset.

Epilepsy

Myoclonic seizures tend to happen on waking or in the early morning. Therefore, the teacher needs to be informed if such episodes have occurred as the child may be tired and inattentive during the first part of the school day.

Children experiencing tonic-clonic, tonic or clonic seizures in school may need a short rest following the seizure but there is no need to call the parents or an ambulance unless this has been previously agreed.

It is important to note that epilepsy is a 'recognised disability' under the DDA, 2002. For example, some children with epilepsy may be entitled to extra time or support in exams because their epilepsy affects their ability to function at the same level as their classmates. If teachers think this may be the case, they should speak to the child's parents and if possible a health or psychology service professional. Schools need to apply to the relevant examining body in adequate time. Guidelines on applying for special adjustments in exams are available from the Joint Council for Qualifications website: www.jcq.org.uk. The implications of epilepsy for a child's education are dealt with in detail later.

All parents and carers should be notified if a seizure has occurred during the school day. If necessary a **seizure diary** or **seizure record sheet** should be completed and sent home with the child at the end of the day. If a child is known to have absence seizures at school, it is particularly important to note when and how frequently these occur as this has implications for how much the child's access to learning may be interrupted or impaired and also the type of treatment best suited to control this type of seizure.

Triggers of seizures

There are many different stimuli that may act as triggers of a seizure, but some are more relevant to schools. This is useful information to find out, because if the school staff are aware of what triggers or provokes a seizure, they can take steps to reduce the likelihood of one occurring. Children who have long warnings are also sometimes able to take steps that avert the development of a full-blown seizure. The school can also support the child if they have the relevant information concerning how best avoidance techniques may be applied. For a very small number of children, who may have 'reflex' epilepsy, their seizures may be triggered by certain sorts of flicker (sunlight, lighting, TV screens or computer monitors), patterned fabrics, music or reading material. Seizures are usually induced by flickers occurring between 5 and 30 times per second.

Ways of minimizing the effects of TV and computer screens:

- Watch the TV in a well-lit room.
- Use high frequency or flicker free screens ($>100Hz$).
- Use a remote control to ensure the child does not come into close proximity to the screen.
- Sit at least two metres from the television, especially for lengthy viewing.

Epilepsy

- View the screen at a slight angle.
- Cover one eye while viewing – this has also been reported as being of benefit to some children.

Use of sunglasses can reduce the susceptibility to seizures in cases where these are triggered by dappled light, such as through trees or on water. However, such types of epilepsy are extremely rare, and are generally well recognized and managed in affected children. Only about 5 per cent of all people with photosensitive epilepsy are sensitive to flashing lights and flicker. Once this type of epilepsy has been diagnosed it is generally responsive to drug treatment, and photosensitivity only becomes an issue if the medication needs to be re-adjusted or the child forgets to take the medicine regularly.

In the remaining significant majority of children, the propensity for seizures is heightened:

- in a stressful situation or in the period immediately following intense concentration or stress
- if the child is extremely tired or has had interrupted sleep
- during high temperature, or when sickening for an illness, e.g. flu (especially in younger children)
- in a pre-menstrual phase (catamenail seizures)
- as a result of alcohol (excess or sudden withdrawal), or drug abuse.

Relaxation exercises can lessen the risk of stress-related seizures, as can the use of certain aromatherapy oils in conjunction with stress management and advice (usually provided through clinical psychology or specialist counselling services).

The following advice forms part of an Epilepsy Policy for schools, reproduced by kind permission of Epilepsy Action. This policy document provides key information to help schools provide effective and appropriate support for children and young people with epilepsy. A complete copy is available from Epilepsy Action.

Medicines

The majority of children with epilepsy take medicine to control their seizures. This medicine is usually taken twice daily outside of school hours. It therefore does not normally raise any issues about storage or legal responsibility of school staff administering medicines.

The only time medicine may be urgently required by a child with epilepsy is when their seizures fail to stop after the usual time, or the child goes into 'status epilepticus'. Status epilepticus is defined as a prolonged seizure or a series of seizures without regaining consciousness in between. This is a medical emergency and is potentially life-threatening. If this occurs, an emergency sedative needs to be administered by a trained member of staff. The sedative is often the drug Diazepam, which is administered rectally, although many children needing

continued on next page

---

emergency medicine are now being prescribed a drug called Midazolam that is administered inside the cheek (see the section on emergency medicine below for more information).

Certain types of medicines taken for epilepsy can have an effect on a child's learning or behaviour. It is important staff are aware of this. If a teacher notices a change in the child's learning or behaviour then the issue should be raised with the child's parents.

Likewise, the child's parents should be encouraged to notify the school if there has been a change in medication administration or type so the school can be aware of potential (transient) changes in the child's learning, attention, vigilance and/or behaviour. It is also important to reschedule formative assessments such as SATs wherever possible if the child has had a change of medication within three weeks of the assessment, and if the child has had a seizure within 24–48 hours of the day of the test or assessment procedure. Dispensation or special examination arrangements can be put in place much more easily prior to the examination or assessment period if arrangements are made that can be acted on with the minimum amount of interruption both to the child or young person concerned and to the school.

Emergency medicines

If a child with epilepsy is likely to require emergency medicines to stop a seizure then it is vital that the parents notify the school before this situation arises. Although it is not a legal requirement for school staff to administer medicines, the school should ensure that a number of staff are trained to administer emergency medicines. Training can be arranged by the School Health Service, the local authority or through an independent training provider. For more information visit www.epilepsy.org.uk or call the Epilepsy Action helpline 0808 800 5050. Many schools have no problem finding staff willing to volunteer to administer emergency medicines.

The two main forms of emergency medicines are rectal Diazepam and buccal Midazolam. As its name suggests, rectal Diazepam is administered rectally. Many parents now choose buccal Midazolam where possible, which is administered inside the cheek. Buccal Midazolam is currently unlicensed for treating epilepsy in children. However, many consultants and some epilepsy specialist nurses prescribe buccal Midazolam due to its obvious advantages. The government's own advice on the use of buccal Midazolam states that if the medicine is used in schools then 'instructions for use must come from the prescribing doctor'.

continued on next page

The above information may appear daunting for some staff, but despite any perceived fears of 'doing the wrong thing' it is essential for schools to have a clear policy and procedure in place to deal with an emergency situation. It is equally essential for all staff to be aware of the school's epilepsy policy. (See section below on legal requirements and responsibilities.)

Guidance from the DfES and Department of Health on administering emergency medicines reassures schools by stating clearly: 'In general, the consequences of taking no action are likely to be more serious than those of trying to assist in an emergency.'

For more information on emergency medicines, and template forms on storing and administrating medicines in schools, see the DfES document, *Managing Medicines in Schools and Early Years Settings* (2005). This document can be downloaded or ordered online at: www.teachernet.gov.uk/medical/ or by calling the DfES order line on 0845 602 2260.

Why schools need an epilepsy policy

It is essential for schools to have an epilepsy policy. Epilepsy Action believes that all children with epilepsy should be given the same opportunities to

continued on next page

achieve their full potential and enjoy the same level of participation in school-life as their friends and classmates.

The DDA, 2002, requires schools and education settings to ensure that all children with disabilities (which includes epilepsy) are not treated 'less favourably' than their classmates.

To help achieve this and fulfil legal requirements, every school or education setting should have a school epilepsy policy. Schools can use an epilepsy policy on its own or as part of another policy, for example the school's health and safety policy, its first aid policy or as part of its Accessible Schools plan.

Some children with epilepsy are prevented from attending school due to prolonged or recurrent absence as a result of their epilepsy. Schools should be prepared to incorporate provision for this in their epilepsy policy. Full guidance on access to education for children with illness or a medical diagnosis can be found in the DfES document 'Access to Education for Children and Young People with Medical Needs.'

Schools should use the information below to develop an epilepsy policy. Each school's policy will be different, but every policy should incorporate the following principles:

continued on next page

Epilepsy

1) This school recognizes that epilepsy is a common condition affecting many children and young people, and welcomes all students with epilepsy;
2) This school believes that every child with epilepsy has a right to participate fully in the curriculum and life of the school, including all outdoor activities and residential trips;
3) This school keeps a record of all the medical details of children with epilepsy and keeps parents updated with any issues it feels may affect the child;
4) This school ensures that all children and staff in the school understand epilepsy and do not discriminate against any children with the condition;
5) This school ensures that all staff fully understand epilepsy and seizure first aid, and that there is at least one member of staff trained to administer emergency medicines in school at all times;
6) This school will work together with children, parents, staff, governors, educational psychologists and health professionals to ensure this policy is successfully implemented and maintained.

Implementing an epilepsy policy

An epilepsy policy should include all the above points and explain how they are to be implemented.

continued on next page

The following is a sample policy from a primary school in England:

Epilepsy Policy – St Egbert's Primary School, Egton, Hatchington, HT1 3RT.

This policy has been written in line with information provided by Epilepsy Action, the Department for Education and Skills, the local education authority, the school health service, the governing body, students and parents.

St Egbert's recognizes that epilepsy is a common condition affecting children and welcomes all children with epilepsy to the school.

St Egbert's supports children with epilepsy in all aspects of school life and encourages them to achieve their fullest potential. This will be done by having a policy in place that is understood by all school staff and the local education authority. This policy ensures all staff receive training on epilepsy and administering emergency medicines. All new staff and supply staff will also receive appropriate training.

What to do when a child with epilepsy joins St Egbert's.

When a child with epilepsy joins St Egbert's, or a current pupil is diagnosed with the condition, the headteacher arranges a meeting with the pupil and their parents to establish how the pupil's epilepsy may

continued on next page

affect their school life. This should include the implications for learning, playing and social development, and out of school activities. They will also discuss any special arrangements the pupil may require, e.g. extra time in exams (see form A for a template questionnaire covering key issues for discussion). With the pupil's and parent's permission, epilepsy will be addressed as a whole-school issue either through assemblies or in the teaching of PSHE or citizenship lessons. Children in the same class as the pupil will be introduced to epilepsy in a way that they will understand. This will ensure the child's classmates are not frightened if the child has a seizure in class.

The school nurse or an epilepsy specialist nurse may also attend the meeting to talk through any concerns the family or headteacher may have, such as whether the pupil requires emergency medicines. The following points in particular will be addressed:

- *Record keeping: During the meeting the headteacher will agree and complete a record of the pupil's epilepsy and learning and health needs. This document may include such issues as: agreeing to administer medicines and any staff training needs (see Form B & C at the end of this document for templates). This record will be agreed by the parents, and the health professional if present, and signed by the parents and headteacher. This form*

continued on next page

will be kept safe and updated when, and where, necessary. Staff will notified of any changes in the pupil's condition through regular staff briefings. This will make staff aware of any special requirements, such as seating the pupil facing the class teacher to help them monitor if the student is having absence seizures and missing part of the lesson.

- **Medicines:** Following the meeting, an individual healthcare plan (IHP) will be drawn up. It will contain some of the information mentioned above and highlight any medicines or first-aid issues of which staff need to be aware (see Form D at the end of this document for a template). In particular it will state whether the pupil requires emergency medicine, and whether the medicine is (rectal Diazepam or buccal Midazolam. It will also contain the names of staff trained to administer that medicine and how to contact these members of staff. If the pupil requires emergency medicines then the school's policy will also contain details of the correct storage procedures in line with the DfES guidance in Managing Medicines in Schools and Early Years Settings (see further reading below).

- **First aid:** First aid for the pupil's seizure type will be included on their IHP and all staff (including ancillary staff) will receive basic training on administering first aid. The following procedure giving basic

continued on next page

first aid for tonic-clonic seizures will be prominently displayed in all classrooms:

1) *Stay calm.*
2) *If the child is convulsing then put something soft under their head.*
3) *Protect the child from injury (remove harmful objects from nearby).*
4) *NEVER try to put anything in their mouth or between their teeth.*
5) *Try to time how long the seizure lasts – if it lasts longer than usual for that pupil or continues for more than five minutes then call medical assistance.*
6) *When the child finishes their seizure, stay with them and reassure them.*
7) *Do not give them food or drink until they have fully recovered from the seizure.*

Sometimes a child may become incontinent during their seizure. If this happens, try and put a blanket around them when their seizure is finished to avoid potential embarrassment. First-aid procedure for different seizure types can be obtained from the school nurse, the pupil's epilepsy specialist nurse or Epilepsy Action.

- ***Learning and behaviour:*** *St Egbert's recognizes that children with epilepsy can have special educational needs because of their condition (see para-*

continued on next page

graphs 7.64–7.67 of the Special Educational Needs Code of Practice). Following the initial meeting, staff will be asked to ensure that the pupil is not falling behind in lessons. If this starts to happen the teacher will initially discuss the situation with the parents. If there is no improvement, then with the school nurse and the school's special needs co-ordinator (SENCO) and the school nurse. If necessary, an Individual Educational Plan will be created, and if the SENCO thinks it appropriate the child may undergo an assessment by an educational psychologist to decide what further action may be necessary.

- *School environment: St Egbert's recognizes the importance of having a school environment that supports the needs of children with epilepsy. A medical room is kept available and equipped with a bed in case a pupil needs supervised rest following a seizure.*

The above epilepsy policy applies equally within the school and, where appropriate, at any outdoor activities organized by the school, including those taking place on the school premises, and residential stays. Any concerns held by the pupil, parent or member of staff will be addressed at a meeting prior to the activity or stay taking place.

The school epilepsy policy in practice

The following example illustrates how a school's epilepsy policy may work in practice. It is important to realize that although a policy may seem detailed and daunting on paper, a lot of its procedures are based on common sense and in practice pose very few problems for the school and its staff on a day-to-day basis.

Jane is playing outside in the sunshine with her friends one morning. Her friend comes running up to the teacher on playground duty. The friend tells the teacher to come quickly as something has happened to Bryony. The teacher finds Bryony at the edge of the hard play area making odd gurgling and grunting sounds. Her arms and legs are jerking and her face has lost all colour. Bryony's teacher gently rolls her on one side and places a folded sweatshirt she has borrowed from another child under her head. She looks round to make sure Bryony's arms and legs will not come into contact with any hard objects. She knows from the school's epilepsy policy not to try and put anything in Bryony's mouth. . . . Gradually the seizure subsides. The teacher stays with Bryony. She realizes that Bryony will need to sleep quietly after the seizure is over. At the very least she will need reassurance of where she is and that everything is all right. . . . Looking at Bryony's school records she noted that although Bryony did not need any emergency medicine, her parents liked to be notified if a seizure happened during the school day. Bryony's father was grateful that the school had not felt the need to call the emergency services and had allowed her to sleep quietly in the medical room for an hour and then to return to class. Although Bryony was tired and had a headache on returning home, there was no seizure recurrence and she attended school as usual the following day.

Scenario adapted from *Epilepsy – a practical guide* by Mike Johnson and Gill Parkinson (2002) published by David Fulton, London.

5 It's a Child's Life

Epilepsy is a chronic condition. It changes over time and its seizures are unpredictable. It is hard for an individual to cope with and difficult to plan for *because* of that unpredictability. Generally, the majority of children with epilepsy lead reasonably unremarkable lives. Only when epileptic seizures change in type or frequency, become out of control or a child goes into status epilepticus does the perspective change. This is much like when any child becomes acutely ill or has an accident requiring hospital treatment. What such events must *not* do is dictate how the child's life should be from then on. Obviously, this last statement is an over-generalization since children's epilepsies can vary on a spectrum between the 'benign' epilepsies of childhood, to the more rare, complex (harder to treat) epilepsies that come from degenerative conditions, or are associated with other complex neurological impairments. Nevertheless, the governing underlying principle should remain the same, i.e. that a good quality of life should worked for, maintained and encouraged as much as and wherever possible.

Epilepsy

We can support this in various ways. The child should be admitted to or remain in a mainstream school. (See Epilepsy Action, 2005 and DfES, 2002.) In a minority of instances where children have very complex, life-threatening or intractable (resistant to treatment) epilepsy, in association with learning difficulties, severe behavioural or psychiatric difficulties and or cerebral palsy, or require high levels of 24-hour medical care, then a more specialist (possible residential) school may be considered. Even if specialist schooling is required, this should not in any way deprive the child of any of the 'good things in life' (Wolfensberger, Thomas and Caruso (1996)).

Despite attending a mainstream school and receiving a good level of support research studies continue to show that many children with epilepsy tend to under-achieve. This can be for a variety of reasons. Epilepsy itself and the effect of anti-epileptic drugs (AEDs) can impair learning and retention of information. Many children with epilepsy are almost *expected* not to perform as well as their peers, so that this expectation of under-achievement by parents, teachers and other professionals can become a self-fulfilling prophecy. Walker and Shorvon (1999) show that there are clear social implications of epilepsy; interrupted schooling, feelings of poor self-worth, insecurities, anxieties and frustration about the school experience all contribute to under-achievement.

The literature also points to parents being over-anxious, overly vigilant and overprotective of their children. Professionals can lose sight of what parents may have gone through emotionally and psychologically before they meet them. Many parents will have had emotional roller-coaster rides with the child's health, access to and treatment by a bewildering variety of services, and experienced very steep learning curves on subjects from DfES rules and regulations through to Benefits Agency and NHS/PCT Budgets/resources for specialist hospital and allied services. We all feel unsupported and lacking in knowledge or confidence, particularly when confronted with a child with one of the more unusual epilepsy syndromes, or when we witness a sudden seizure for the first time.

Professionals should not be afraid to admit their uncertainties and share this with parents and colleagues while being very clear about what they do know. Parents are an often overlooked but invaluable source of information which would be of use and value to professionals involved in assessment and education of their child. However, they must have confidence that the person they are dealing with has clear expertise in their area of professionalism. Joint working helps parents to feel involved and empowered as partners in the care of their child.

The following are considered to have a significant bearing on whether a child's quality of life contains 'good things' in it:

- over-indulgence of behaviour normally regarded as inappropriate or unacceptable
- the child's own self-perception and level of self-esteem

- attitudes of others (siblings, friends, relatives, etc.)
  a) to the child
  b) to the epilepsy
- self expectation and expectation of others e.g. development of over-dependence and conceptualization of self as 'ill'
- child and family access to school and the local community
  a) personally
  b) socially
  c) academically
  d) post-school (careers, HE (Higher Education) FE (Further Education), meaningful employment)
- issues relating to overprotection
- over-vigilance.

A sense of protection is something we all feel when children are young and when we feel they are vulnerable to unpleasant external influences that might put them at risk of self-harm or harm from others. Children who experience seizures which are unpredictable in time and frequency of onset, seizures which are not preceded by a warning aura or 'pre-ictal period' of some kind such as headache or disturbed sleep are likely to be at a higher risk of self-injury (especially in atonic seizures or 'drop attacks') than other children with well-controlled seizures or those which only occur at night. Therefore, the instinct to protect the child tends to be over-magnified as the risk – perceived or otherwise – increases (see discussion by Johnson and Parkinson, 2002).

These feelings can be reduced significantly through thoughtful risk-management. The child's concerns are reduced because they know the situation is under control and the adult's are alleviated because they have systems in place which can cope with such an eventuality if and or when it arises. Quality of life can be seriously diminished for parents, child, siblings and peers if space and time are not built into the child's life-style so that serious risk is *minimized* and *controlled*, yet the child is still allowed to learn to live with the day-to-day risks that we all must learn to cope with.

A child for whom the epilepsy has been used as an excuse for their behaviour or way of gaining 'special treatment' because they have 'suffered so much . . .', may also be deprived of a reasonable quality of life because they are no longer able to form or maintain social relationships, visit places that require certain codes of conduct or share activities with friends and family which demand cooperation and adherence to certain (even simple) social rules. Sometimes, when the epilepsy is controlled, the underlying causes defined and, where possible, treated, the legacy of over-indulgence remains. In order to help such children and their families, one needs to work with and support the family as a whole. This is important as over-indulgence, conscious or otherwise, can occur for many reasons that need to be worked through before the child *and* the family can move forward.

Self-identity and self-image may understandably have a negative impact on self-esteem and self-worth. There is a recognized risk of adolescents developing depressive or anxiety-related illnesses as a reaction to or secondary development of their epilepsy. Accepting a diagnosis of epilepsy is hard, both for the child and the family. The news can be devastating for example when the child is felt to be recovering well from an acute illness, injury or surgery, only to be told that the child has epilepsy too. People react in different ways (as discussed earlier), but for the individual child or young person, on the threshold of life, the news can be a great shock which can be immediate or not really become obvious until months or even years later. Anger, shock and frustration at the changes imposed on their lives, knowledge that skills may have been lost and an overwhelming feeling of failure and injustice can compound an already difficult situation.

However, there are people and services (see Useful addresses) that can help. Some of these people, such as counsellors, epilepsy liaison nurses and social workers, will have experience of supporting people through the difficult early stages of confirmation of diagnosis, acceptance and adjustment. Some of the specialist epilepsy charities run helplines, websites, regional and district meetings and self-help groups. These can be an invaluable source of help and support. They can be arenas where parents, carers and professionals can meet specialists and others with epilepsy to compare notes and ask questions they might feel unable to voice in a more formal setting.

In an educational or therapeutic setting, low self-esteem and feelings of poor self-worth can be seen when the individual shows some of the following:

- lethargy
- irritability for no apparent reason
- irrational mood swings
- low mood
- social withdrawal
- non-submission of coursework, or homework which is spasmodic or unexpected
- evasiveness
- absconding
- emotional liability, e.g. cries easily
- proneness to anger and intolerance of others.

(Johnson and Parkinson, 2002)

Specialist psychology (hospital-, community- and GP-based) services together with counselling (GP- or hospital-based) can significantly improve the outlook of individuals finding it difficult to come to terms with or adjust to changes in the nature of their epilepsy.

Adolescence can be more fraught than usual, since the young person is struggling to come to terms not only with epilepsy but also with the changes in his or her own body, and the psychosocial changes that accompany an increasing desire for independence and personal autonomy. They may also start to realize that epilepsy brings new implications and possible lifestyle restrictions. They may take the role of a subservient or 'sick' child, or conversely rebel against this condition which they may feel places shackles upon their life. It is the responsibility of everyone involved in the care and support of young people with epilepsy, to ensure that a sense of inclusion and independence is fostered – one that *ena*bles rather than *disa*bles the young person from participating in activities with friends, family, school and within his or her local community.

Young people with additional problems such as learning difficulties, autism and physical disability pose more complex challenges. Such young people should not be excluded from consideration of quality of life-related issues and wherever possible they too should be encouraged to take decisions and assume responsibility for their treatment management, choice of participation in social and other non-academic pastimes. Choice of activity should not be limited simply because the individual has epilepsy. We should aspire towards a socially as well as educationally inclusive society where all children are equally valued regardless of their disability.

References

Department for Education and Skills. *Accessible Schools: Planning to increase access for schools for disabled pupils*, www.dfes.gov.uk/sen. 2002.

Epilepsy Action. *Epilepsy and Inclusive Education: A policy for change*, www.epilepsyaction.org.uk. 2005.

Johnson, M. and Parkinson, G. *Epilepsy: A practical guide.* London, David Fulton. 2002.

Walker, M. and Shorvon, S. D. *The British Medical Association Family Doctor Guide to Epilepsy.* London, Dorling Kindersley. 1999.

Further Information

Legal requirements and responsibilities

The following information is taken from the DfES document *Managing Medicines in Schools and Early Years Settings* (2005). It aims to highlight the importance of having a clear school epilepsy policy and help staff understand their responsibility in ensuring the safety of a child with epilepsy in their school. It is also reproduced in Epilepsy Action's Epilepsy Policy for Schools (Epilepsy Action 2005, p. 12).

The general guidance for ensuring the health and safety of children in schools states that it is the employer's responsibility (under the Health and Safety at Work Act 1974) to make sure schools have a health and safety policy which includes procedures for supporting children with medical needs. It is also the employer's responsibility to

continued on next page

make sure that they have taken out Employer's Liability Insurance and that this insurance provides full cover for school staff acting within full scope of their employment i.e. 'duty of care'. In community and voluntary-controlled schools the LEA is usually the employer, while in foundation and voluntary-aided schools, staff are employed by the governing body.

In the day-to-day management of children's medical needs, parents should give schools information about their child's condition, including any relevant details from the child's GP, consultant or epilepsy specialist nurse. Parents are also responsible for supplying any information about the medicine their child needs and providing details of any change to the child's prescription or support required.

There is no legal duty requiring school staff to administer medicine. However, schools should consider this issue as part of their accessibility planning duties. Staff are usually happy to volunteer for training to administer emergency medicines. Some proactive schools even require support staff to be trained in administering emergency medicines as part of their role (full roles and responsibilities are detailed in *Managing Medicines in Schools and Early Years Settings*).

Further reading

The following publications provide useful practical and statutory advice for schools. Those marked with an asterisk (*) are considered essential reading.

DfES. *Special Educational Needs Code of Practice*. Nottingham. 2001.*

DfES. *Managing Medicines in Schools and Early Year Settings*. Nottingham. 2005.*

DfES. *Accessible Schools: Summary Guidance*. Nottingham. 2002.

Epilepsy Action. *Levelling the playing field: a report on epilepsy and education*. Leeds. 2005.* (Unpublished.)

Epilepsy Action. *A Policy for Schools*. Leeds. 2005.

Epilepsy Action. *Positive Action in Education*. Leeds. 2005.*

Hull Learning Services. *Supporting Children with Epilepsy*. London. David Fulton, 2004.

Hull Learning Services. *Supporting Children with Medical Needs*. London. David Fulton, 2002.

Johnson, M. and Parkinson, G. *Resource materials for Teachers: Epilepsy – a practical guide*. London. David Fulton, 2002.*

Wolfensberger, W., Thomas, S. and Caruso, G. (1996) Some of the universal 'good things in life' which the implementation of social role valorisation can be expected to make more accessible to devalued people. SRV/VRS 2(2): 12–14.

Acknowledgements

The example of the school epilepsy policy in practice was adapted from a case study in Johnson and Parkinson, 2002.

Useful addresses

Department for Education and Skills
(publications centre)
PO Box 5050
Annesley
Nottingham
NG15 0DL
Tel: 0845 60 222 60
Web: www.dfespublications.gov.uk

Epilepsy Action
New Anstey House
Gate Way Drive
Yeadon
Leeds
LS19 7XY
Tel: 0113 210 8800
Fax: 0113 391 0300
Helpline: 0808 800 5050
Email: epilepsy@epilepsy.org.uk
Web: www.epilepsy.org.uk

Epilepsy Scotland
48 Govan Road
Glasgow
G51 1JL
Tel: 0141 427 4911
Fax: 0141 419 1709
Email: enquiries@ epilepsyscotland.org.uk
Web: www.epilepsyscotland.gov.uk

Epilepsy Wales
PO Box 4168
CF14 0WZ
Tel: 029 2075 5515
Helpline: 0845 741 3774
Email: epilepsywales@aol.com
Web: www.epilepsy-wales.co.uk

Joint Council for Qualifications
Veritas House
125 Finsbury Pavement
London
EC2A 1NQ
Web: www.jcq.org.uk

**British Complementary Medicines Association
(BCMA)**
PO Box 5122
Bournemouth
BH8 0WG
Tel: 0845 345 5977
Web: www.bcma.co.uk

Useful forms

The following are template forms that may be useful when developing a school epilepsy policy and are reproduced by kind permission of Epilepsy Action (2005).

Form A – Parental questionnaire for students with epilepsy

Form B – Parental agreement for school to administer medicine

Form C – Staff training record – administration of medicines

FORM A – Parental questionnaire for students with epilepsy

This questionnaire should be completed by the child's parents or primary carer and headteacher and the child or young person where this is feasible.

/ Delete as appropriate.

Name: ....

Date of birth: ....

Class/form teacher: ....

What type of seizure/s does your child/you have? (If you know what they're called)

....

How long do they last?

....

What first aid is appropriate?

....

....

....

How long will your child/you need to rest following a seizure?

....

Epilepsy

Are there any factors that you have noted that you feel might trigger a seizure?

....

....

Does your child have any warning before a seizure occurs?

....

What is the name of your child's/your medicine and how much is each dose?

....

How many times a day does your child/do you take medicine?

....

Are there any activities that you feel may require particular precautions?

....

....

Does your child have any other medical conditions?

....

....

Is there any other relevant information you feel the school should be aware of?

....

....

FORM B – Parental agreement for school or setting to administer medicine

The school will not give your child medicine unless this form is completed and the school has a policy for (named) staff to administer medicine.

Name ....
of school: ....

Date: ....

Class/form: ....

Child's name: ....

Medical condition or illness: ....

Name and strength of medicine: ....
....

Expiry date: ....

When to be given: ....

Dosage and method of administration: ....
....

Any side-effects school needs to know about:
....

Epilepsy

Procedure to take in an emergency:

....

Number of tablets/quantity to be given to school:

....

NOTE: Medicines must be in the original container as dispensed by the pharmacy.

Daytime phone number of parent or adult contact:

....

Name and phone number of GP:

....

Agreed review date to be initiated by
[name of member of staff]:

....

The above information is, to the best of my knowledge, accurate at the time of writing and I give consent to school staff administering medicine in accordance with the school policy. I will inform the school immediately, in writing, if there is any change in dosage or frequency of the medicine or if the medicine is stopped.

Parent's signature: ....

Print name: ....

Date: ....

FORM C – Staff training record/administration of medicines

/ Delete as appropriate.

Name of school: ....

Name of staff: ....

Occupation/job title: ....

Type of training received: ....

Date training completed: ....

Training provided by: ....

I confirm that [name of member of staff]

....

has received the training detailed above and agrees
to carry out any necessary treatment.
I recommend that the training is updated
[state how often].

....

121

Epilepsy

Trainer's signature: ....

Date: ....

I confirm I have received the training detailed above.

Staff signature:...

Date: ....

Suggested review date: ....